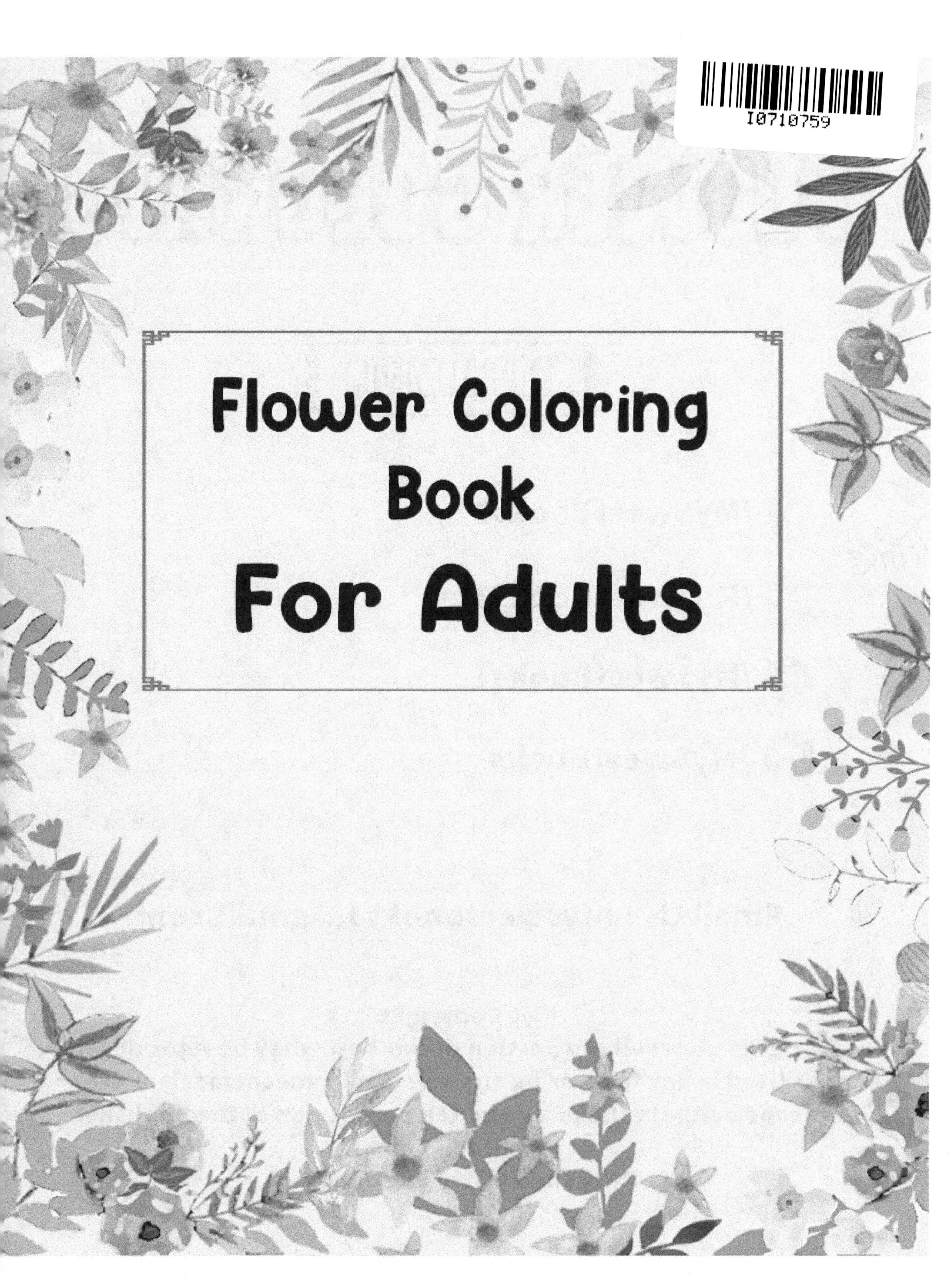

Flower Coloring
Book
For Adults

FLOWER COLORING

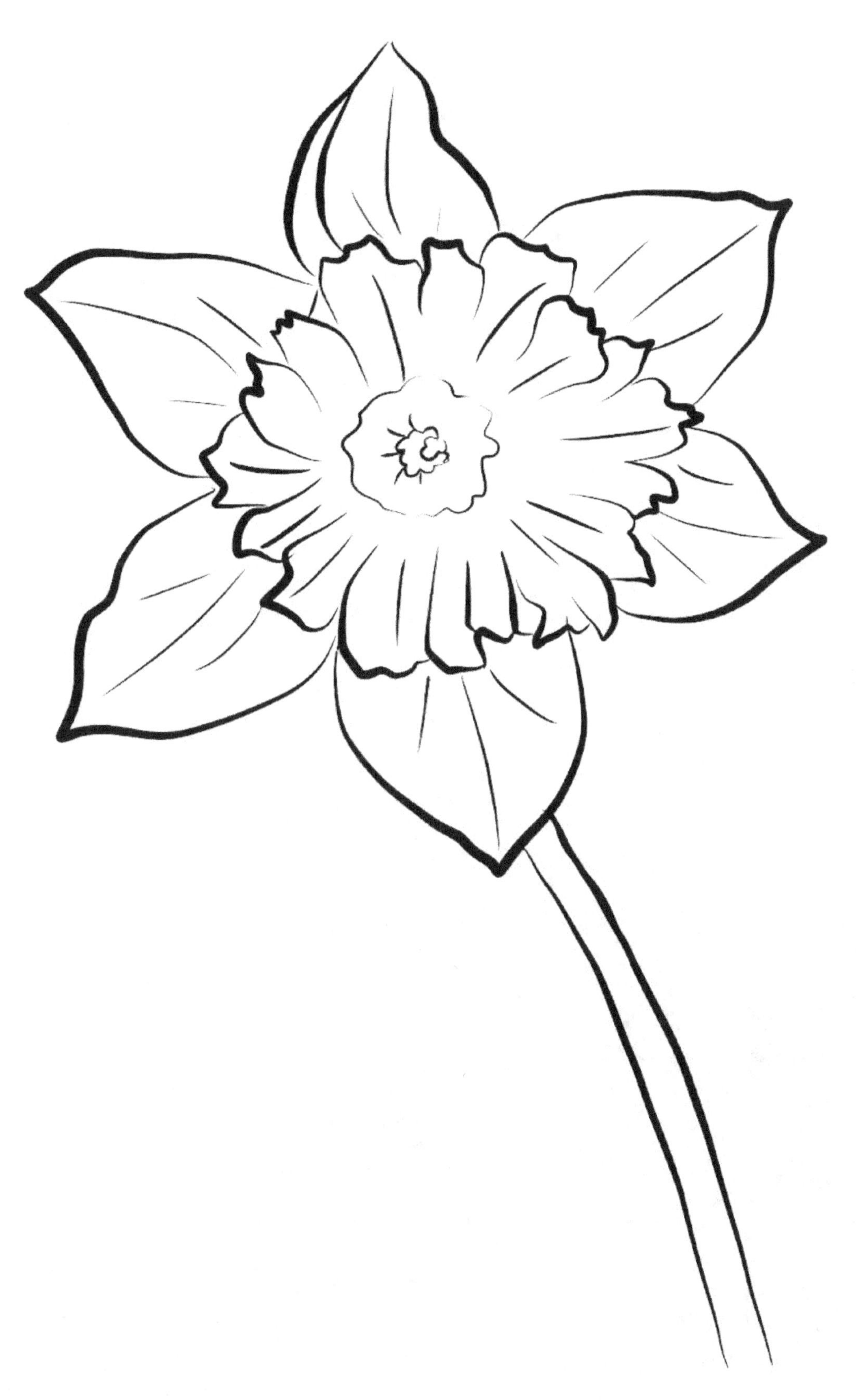

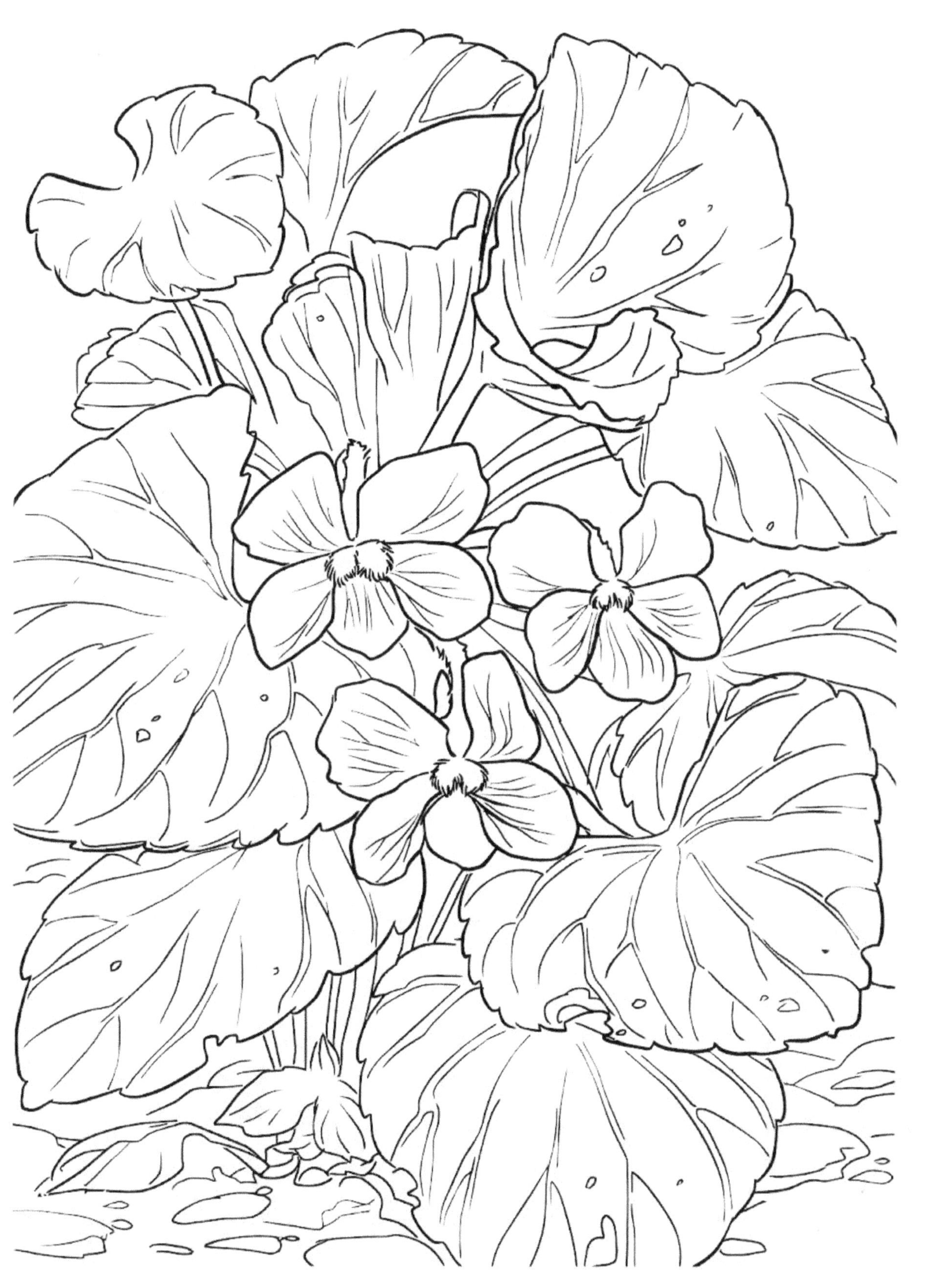

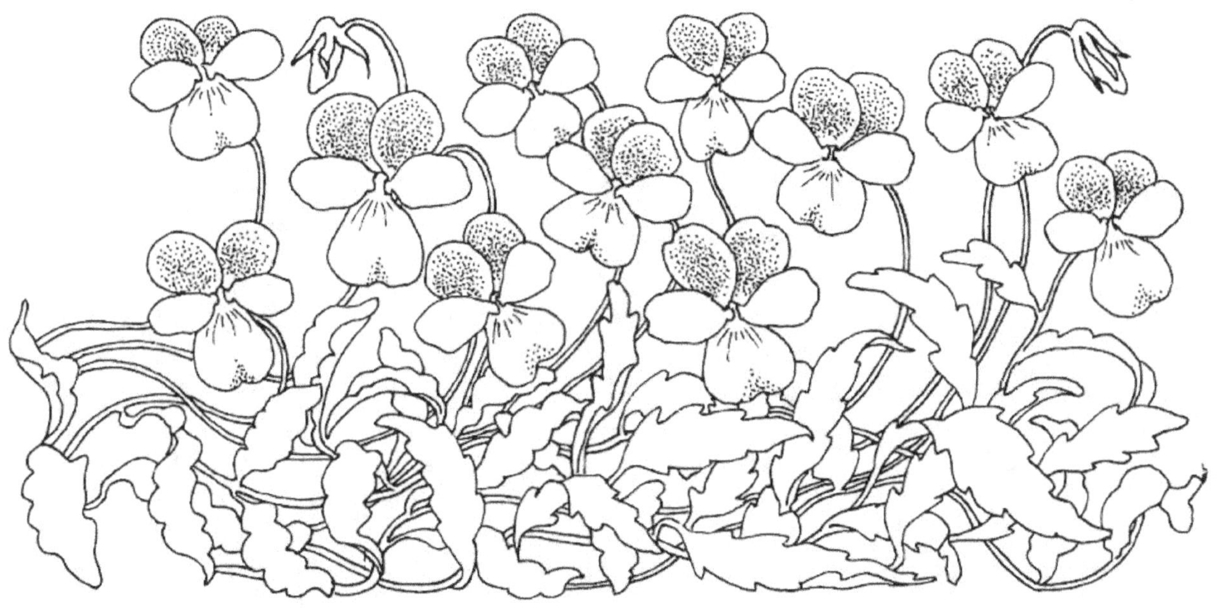

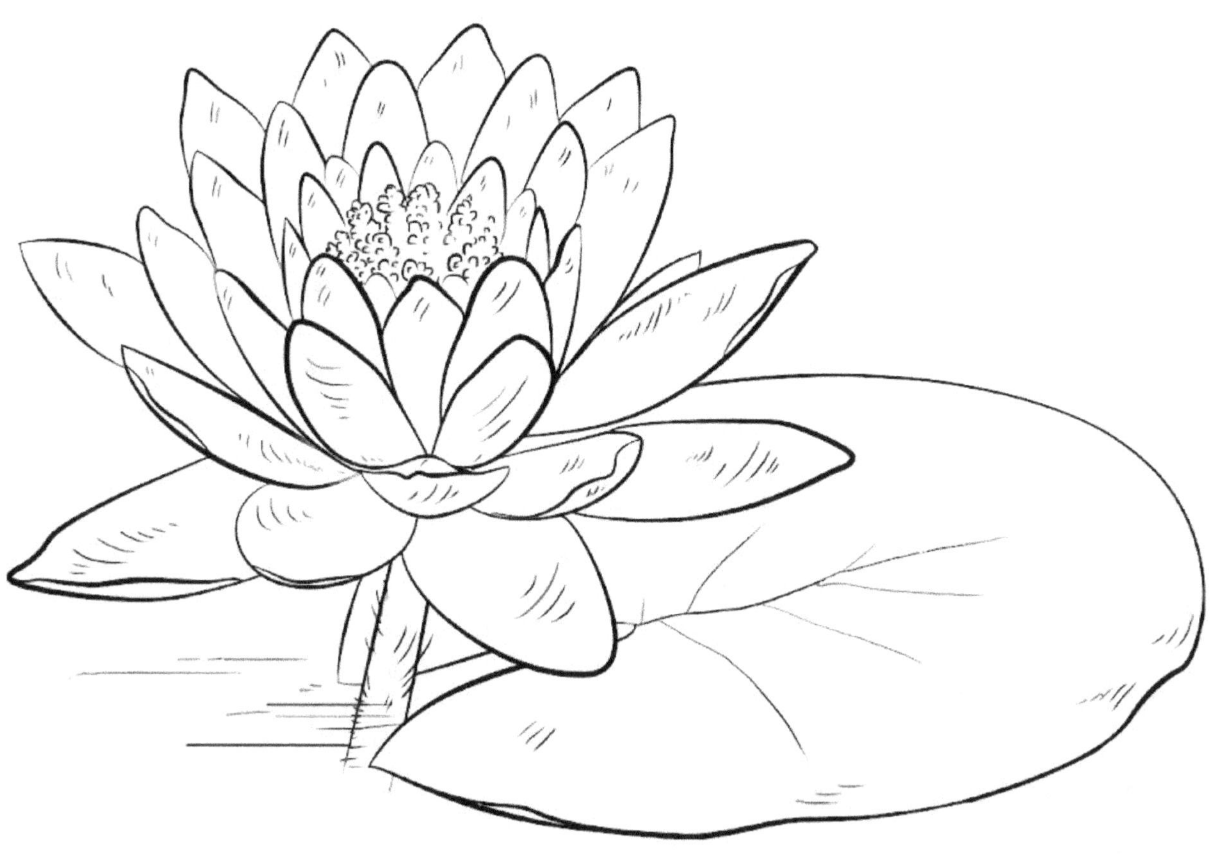

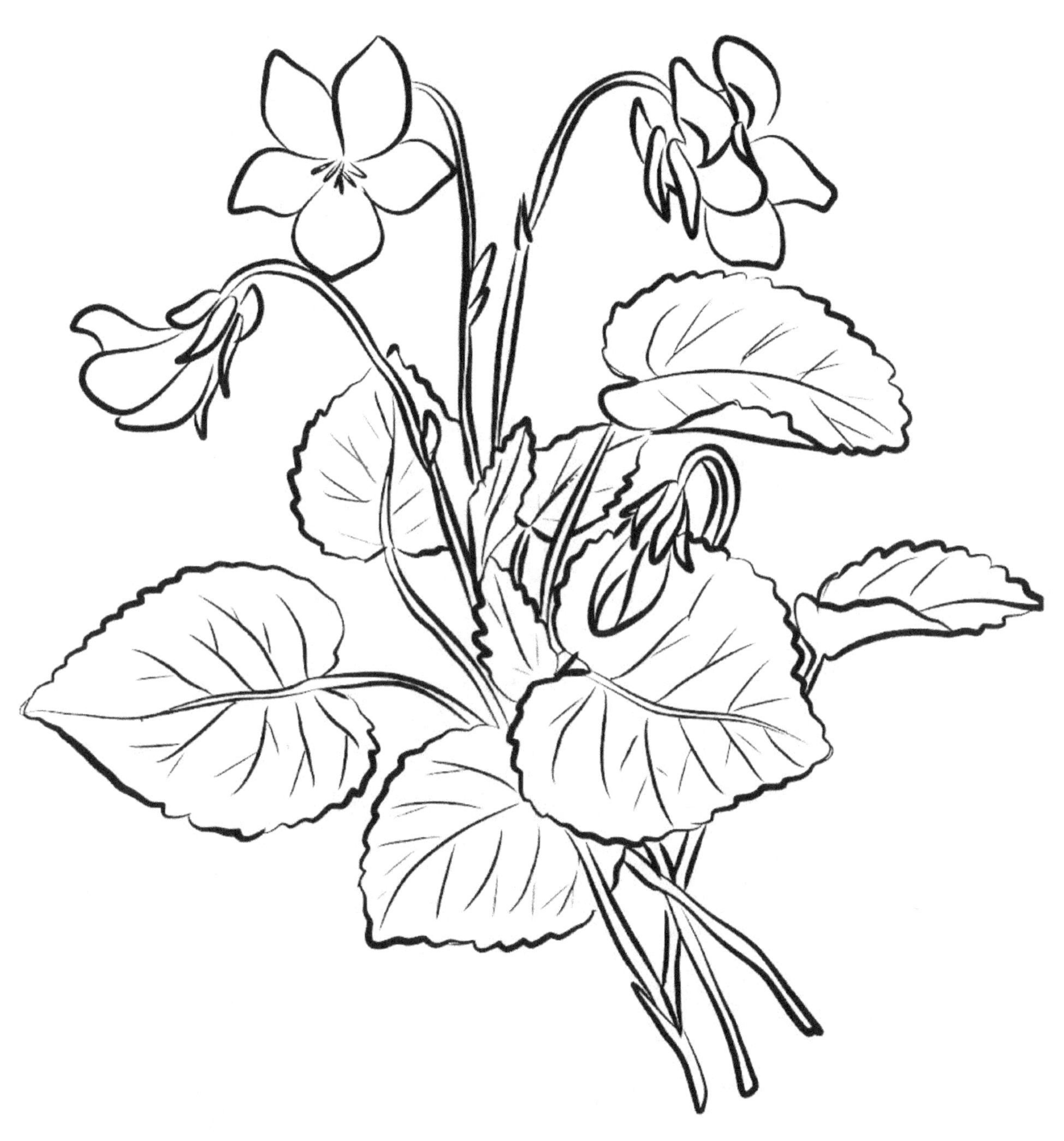

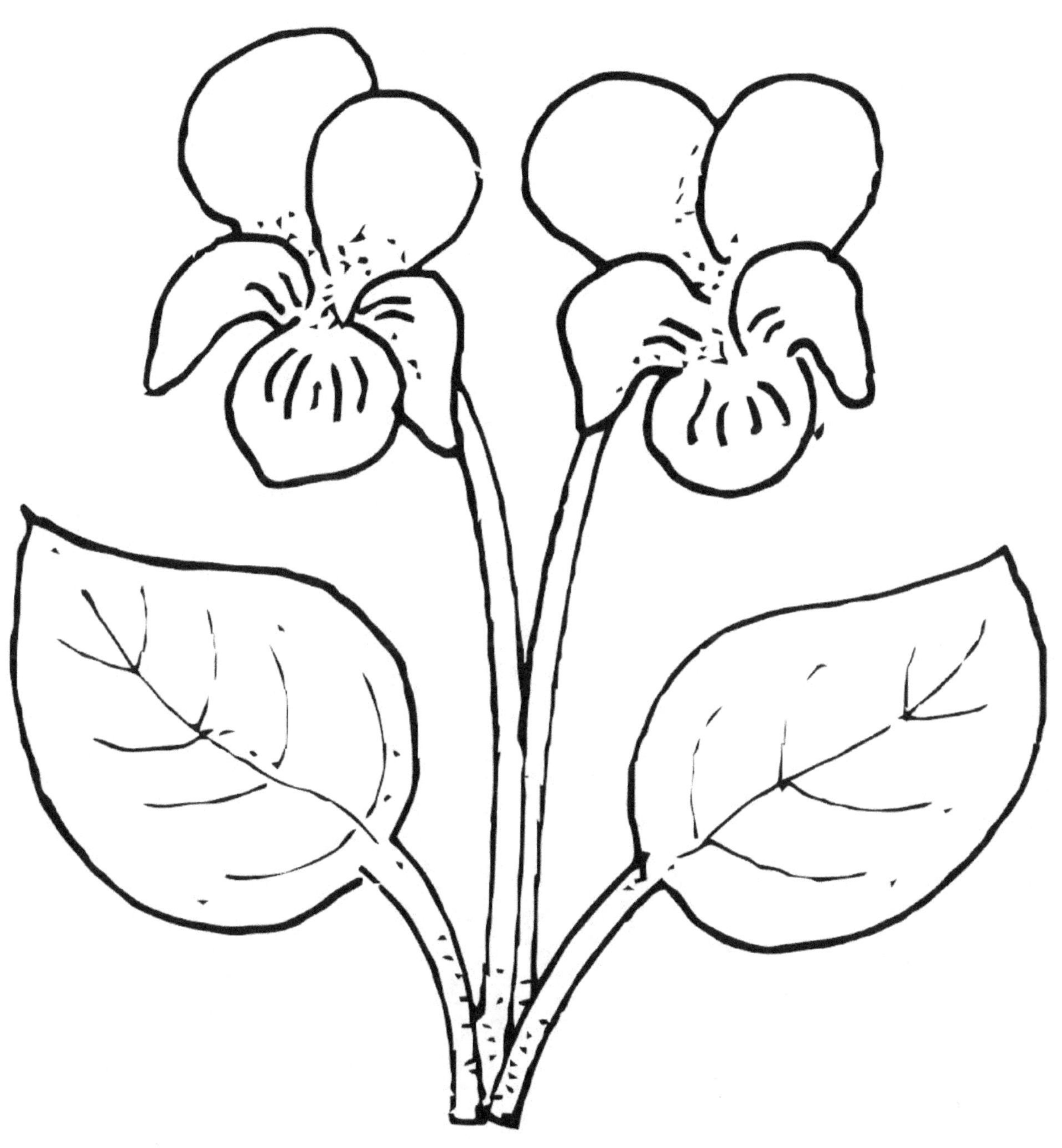

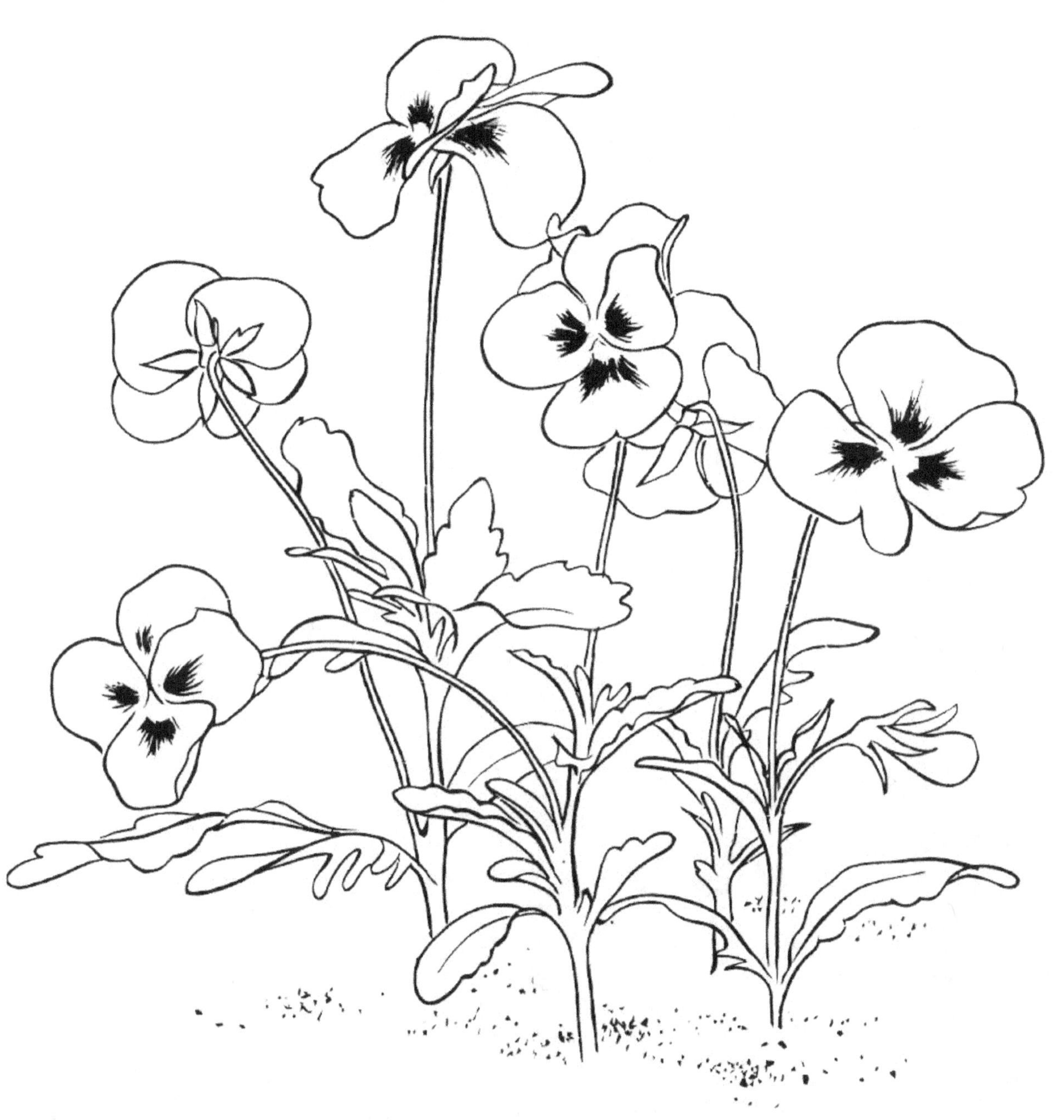

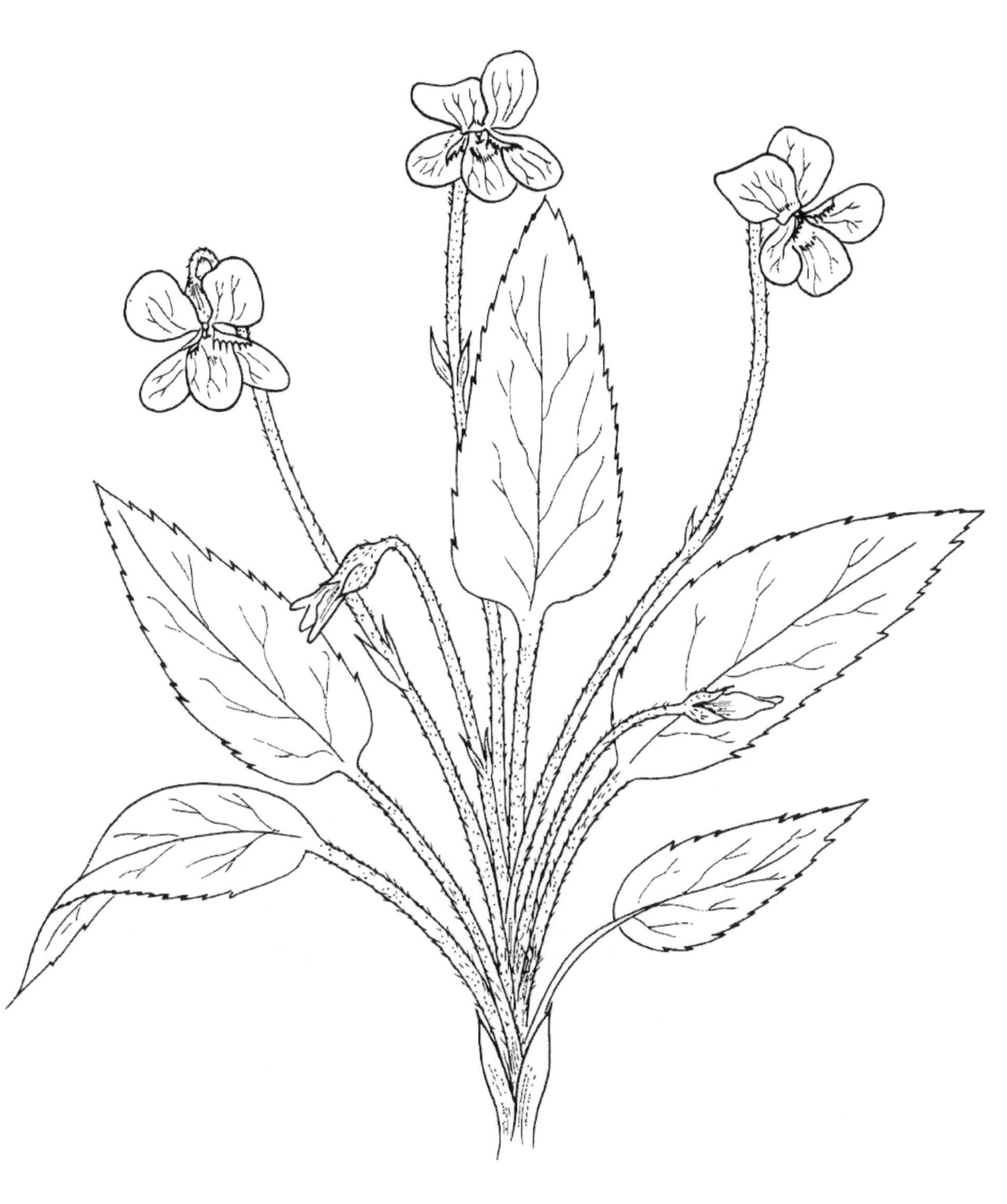

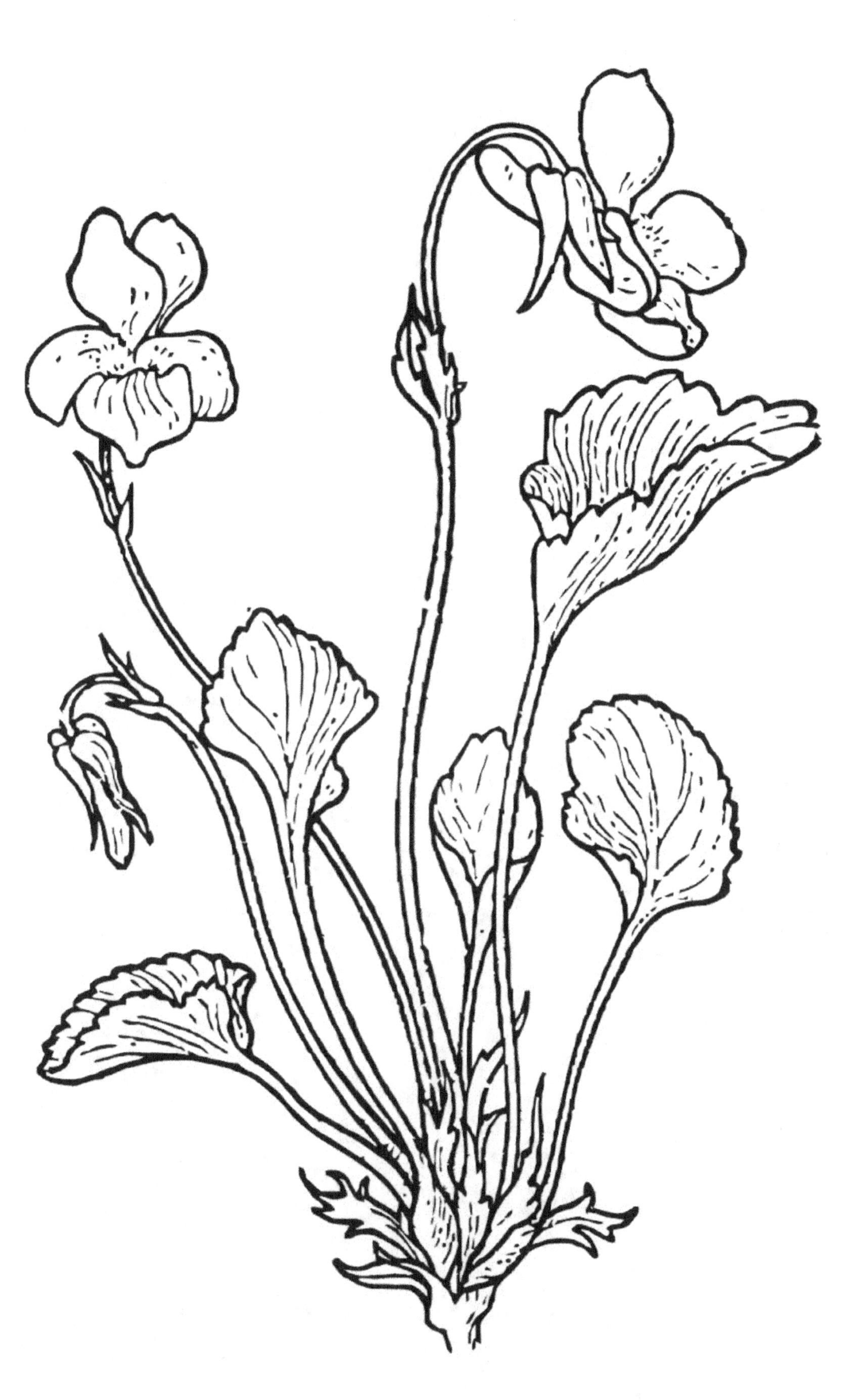

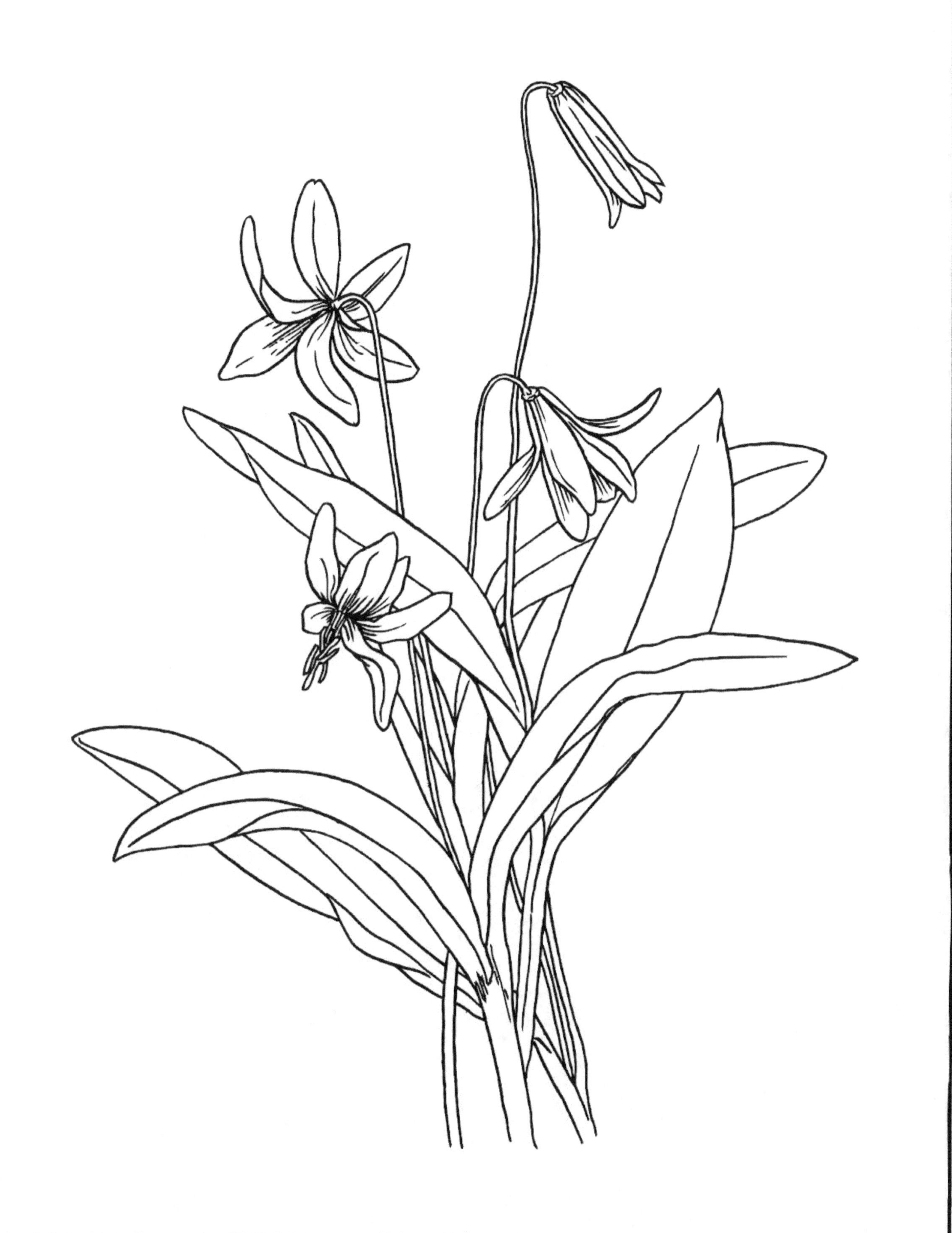

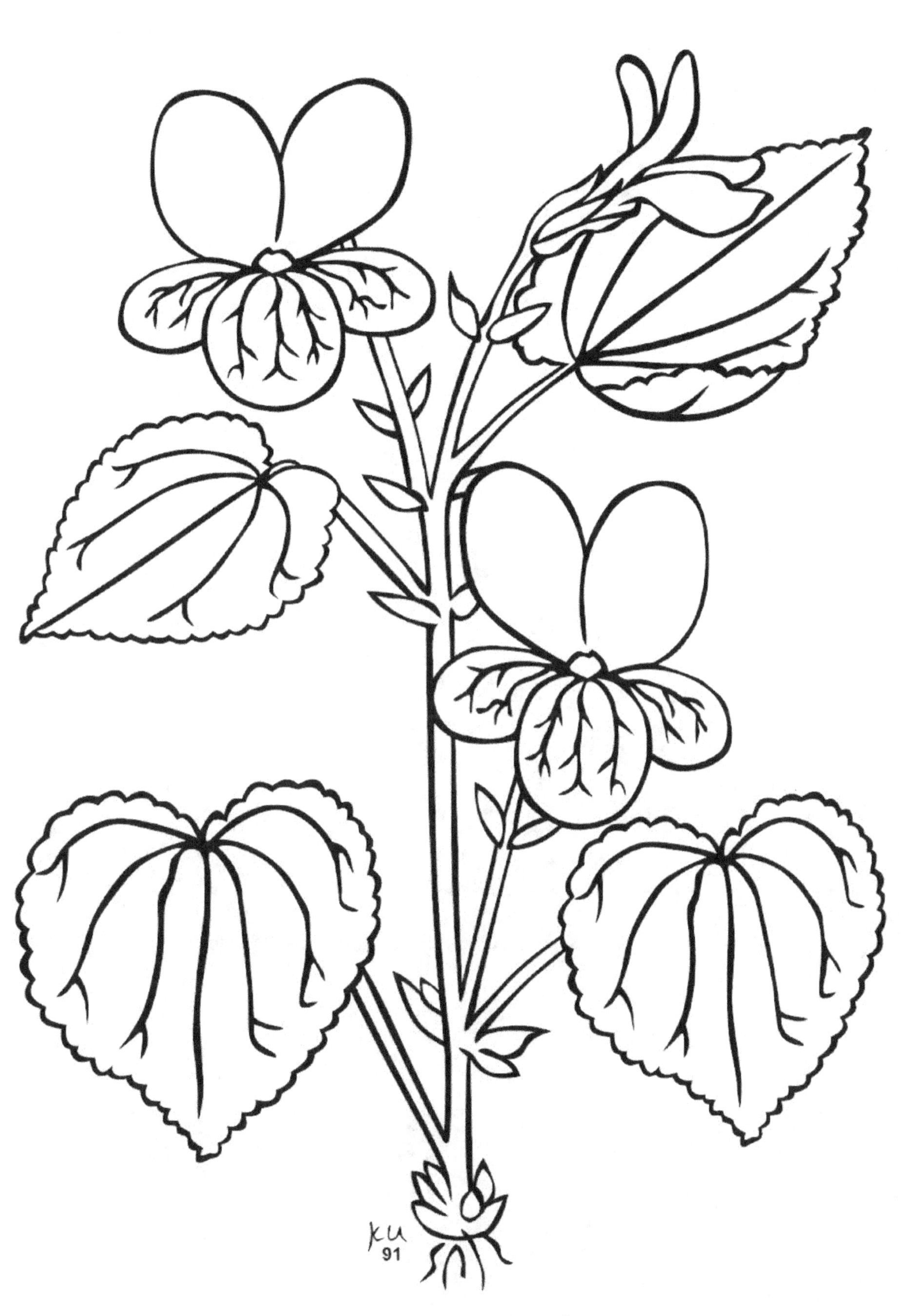

ku
91

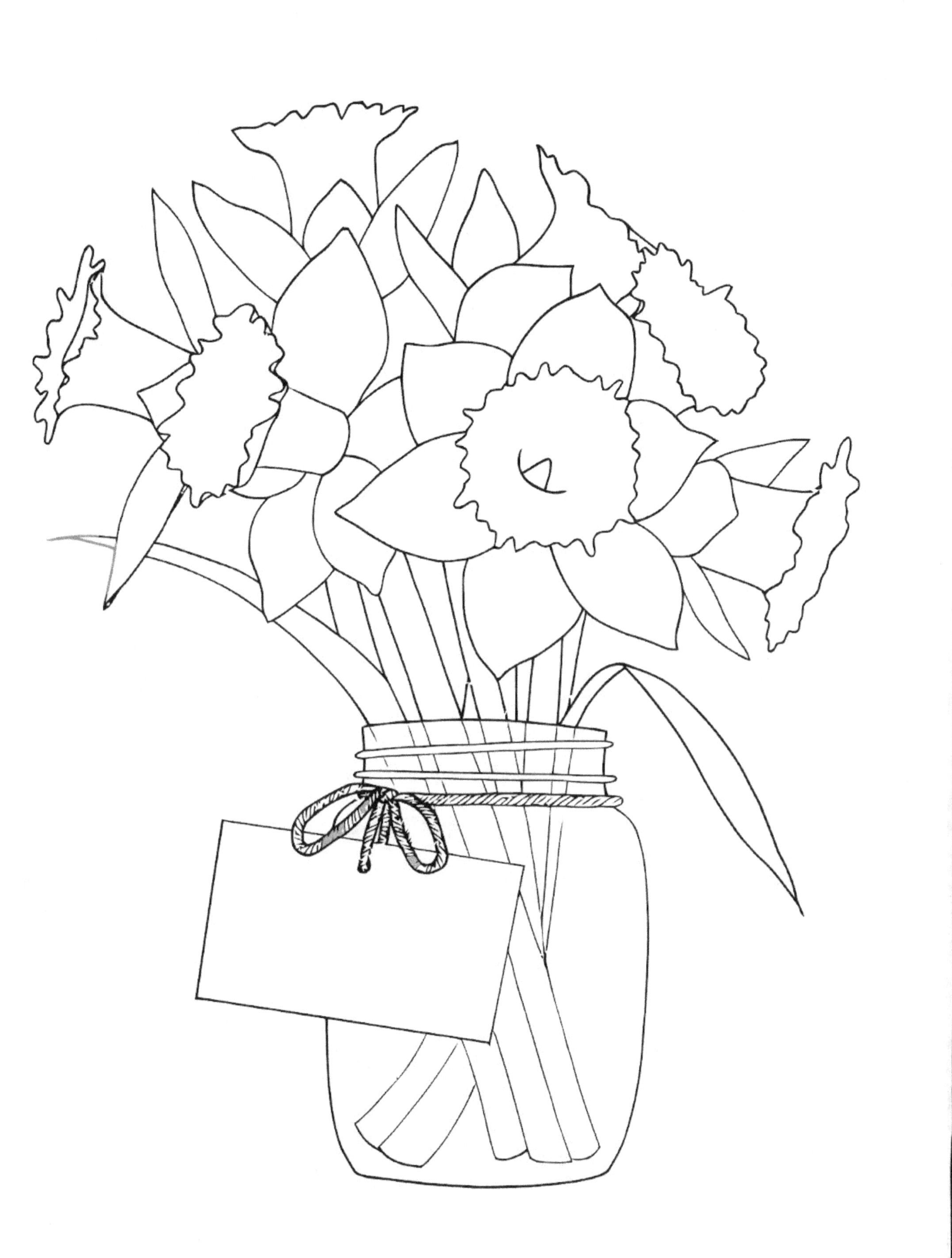

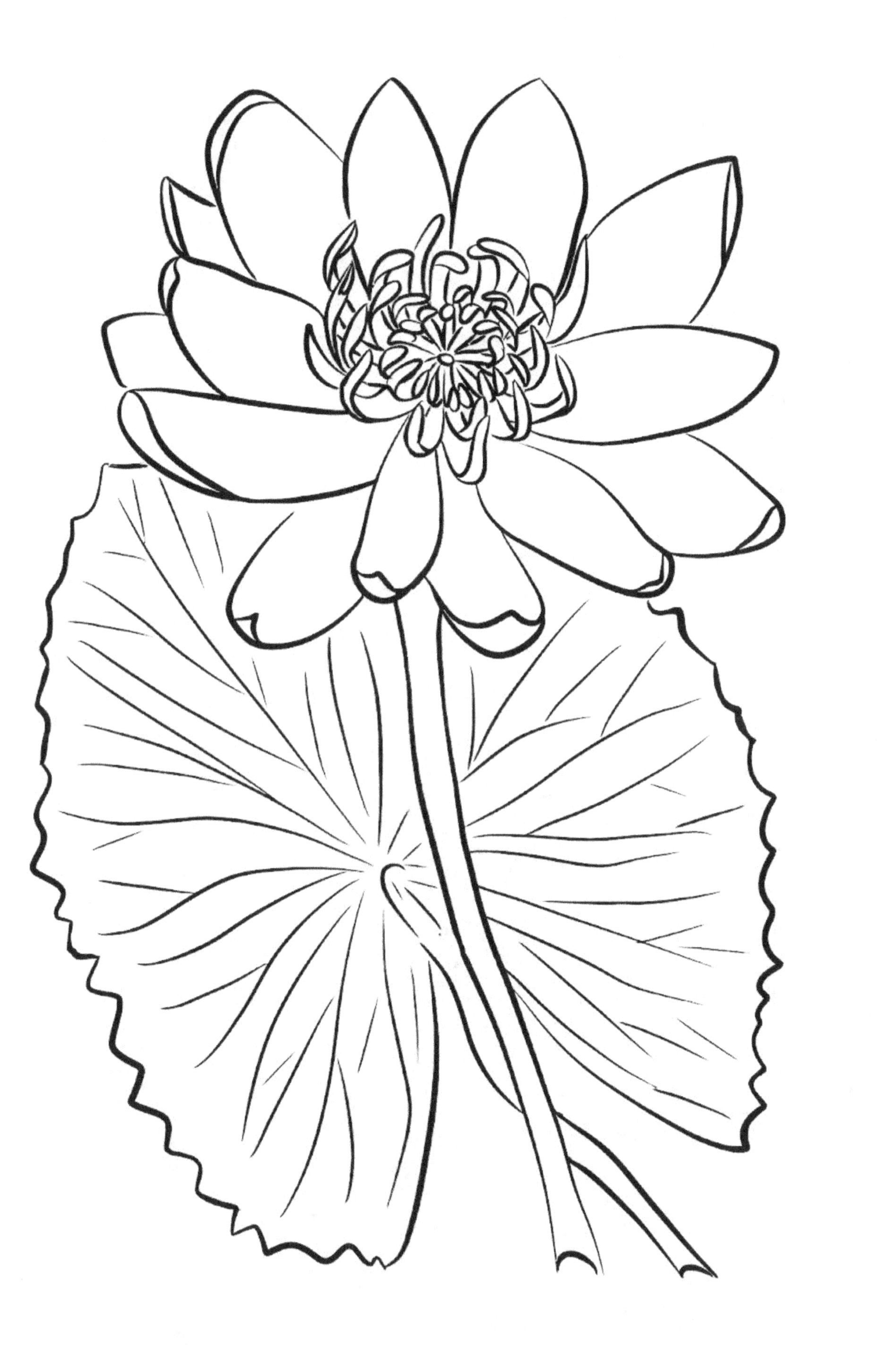

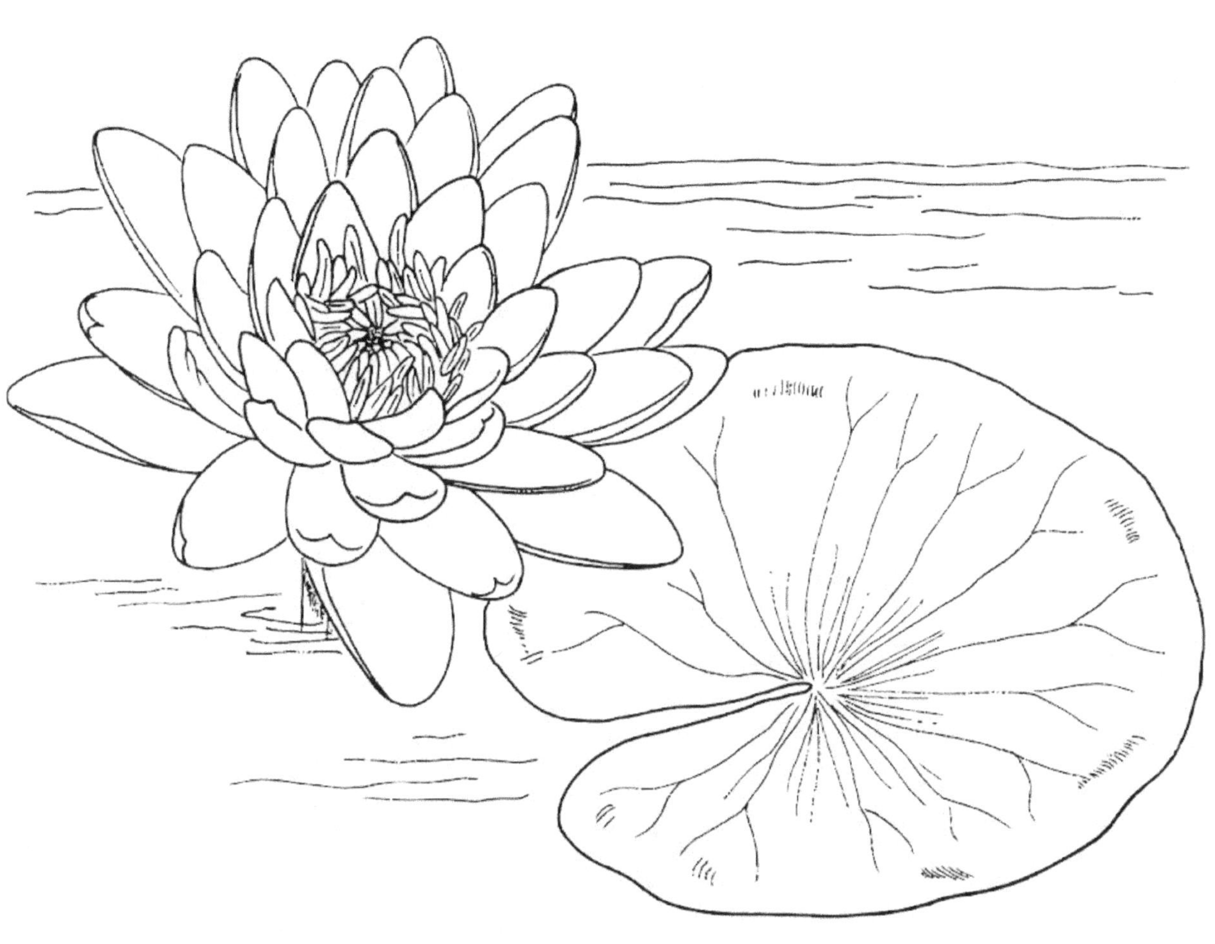

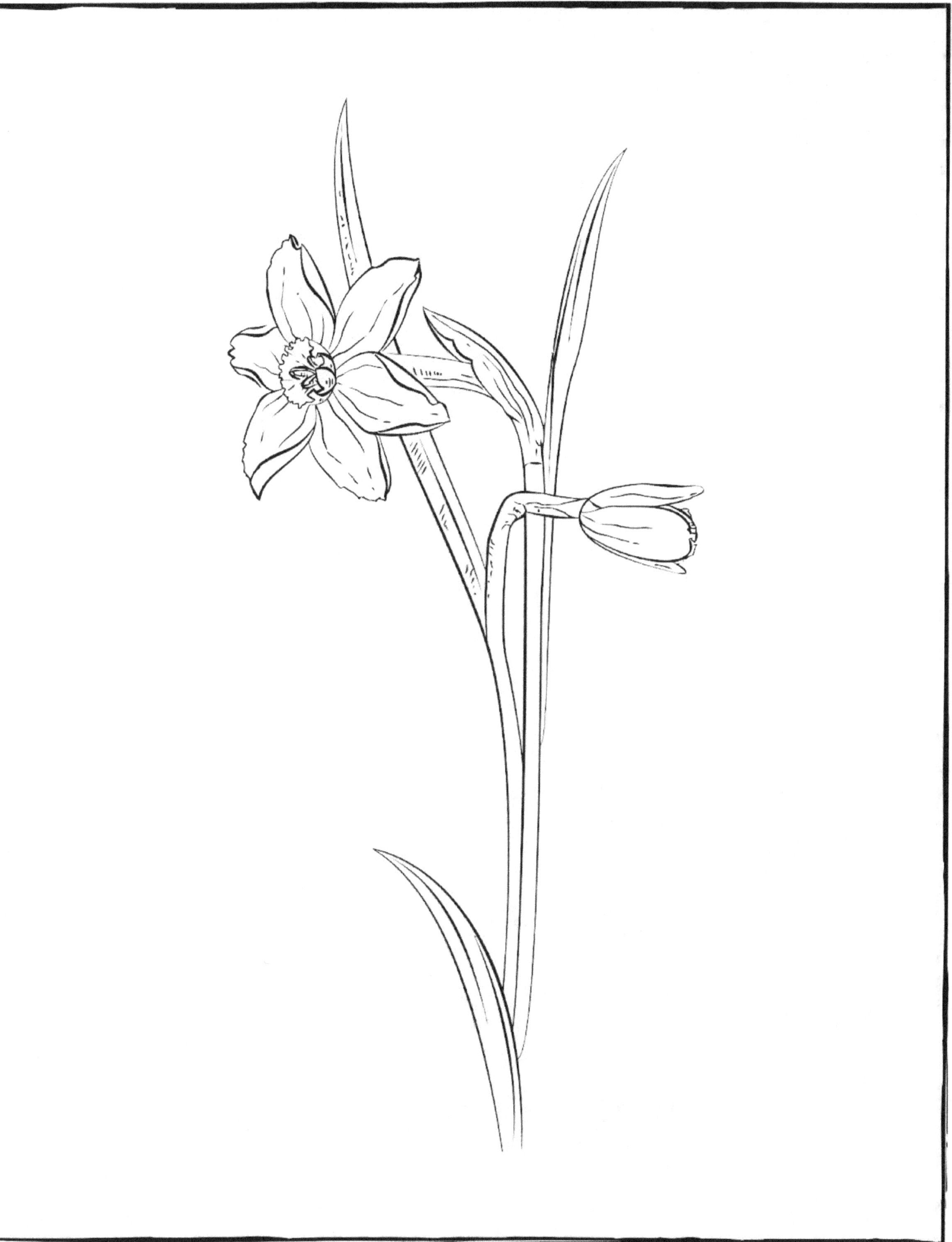

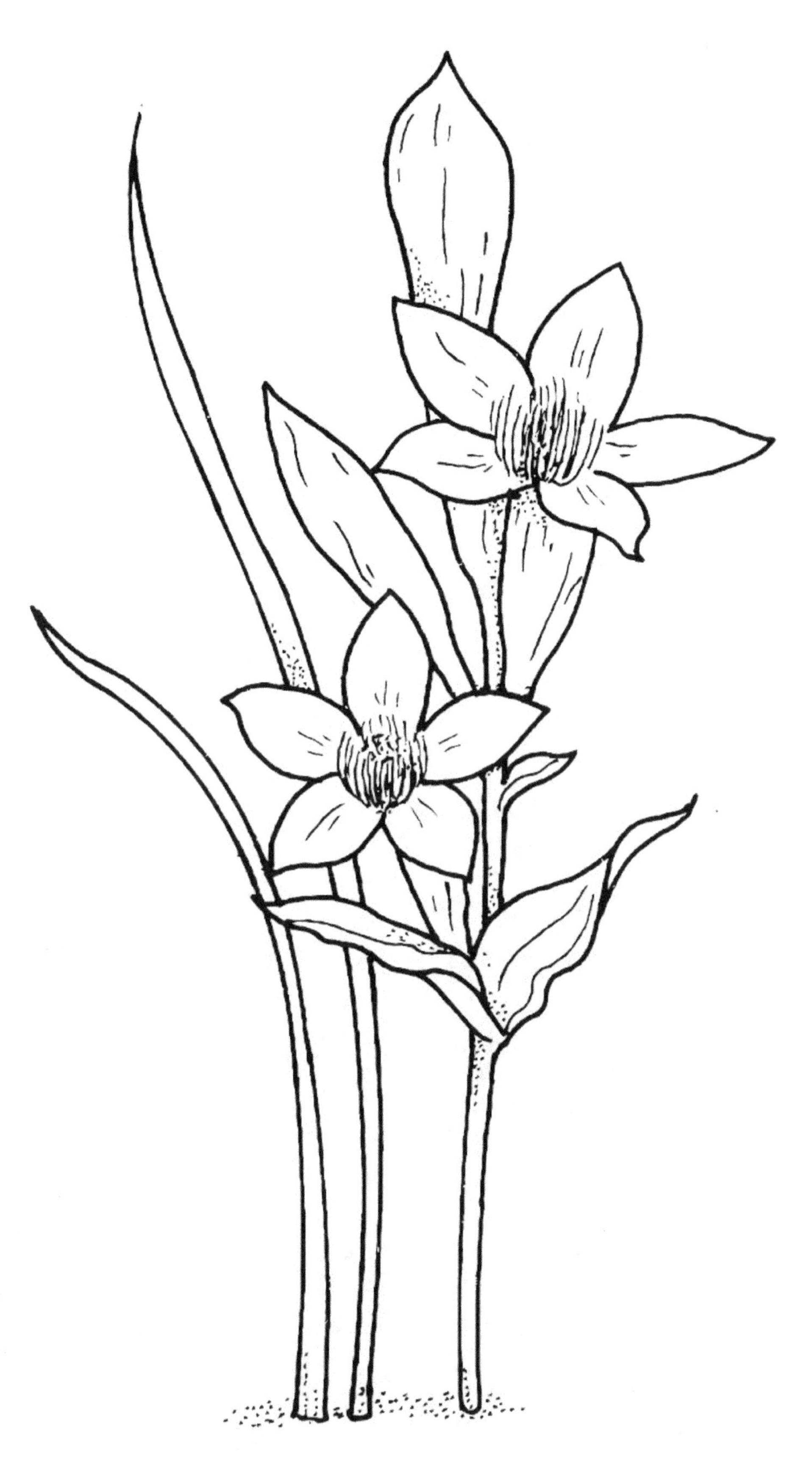

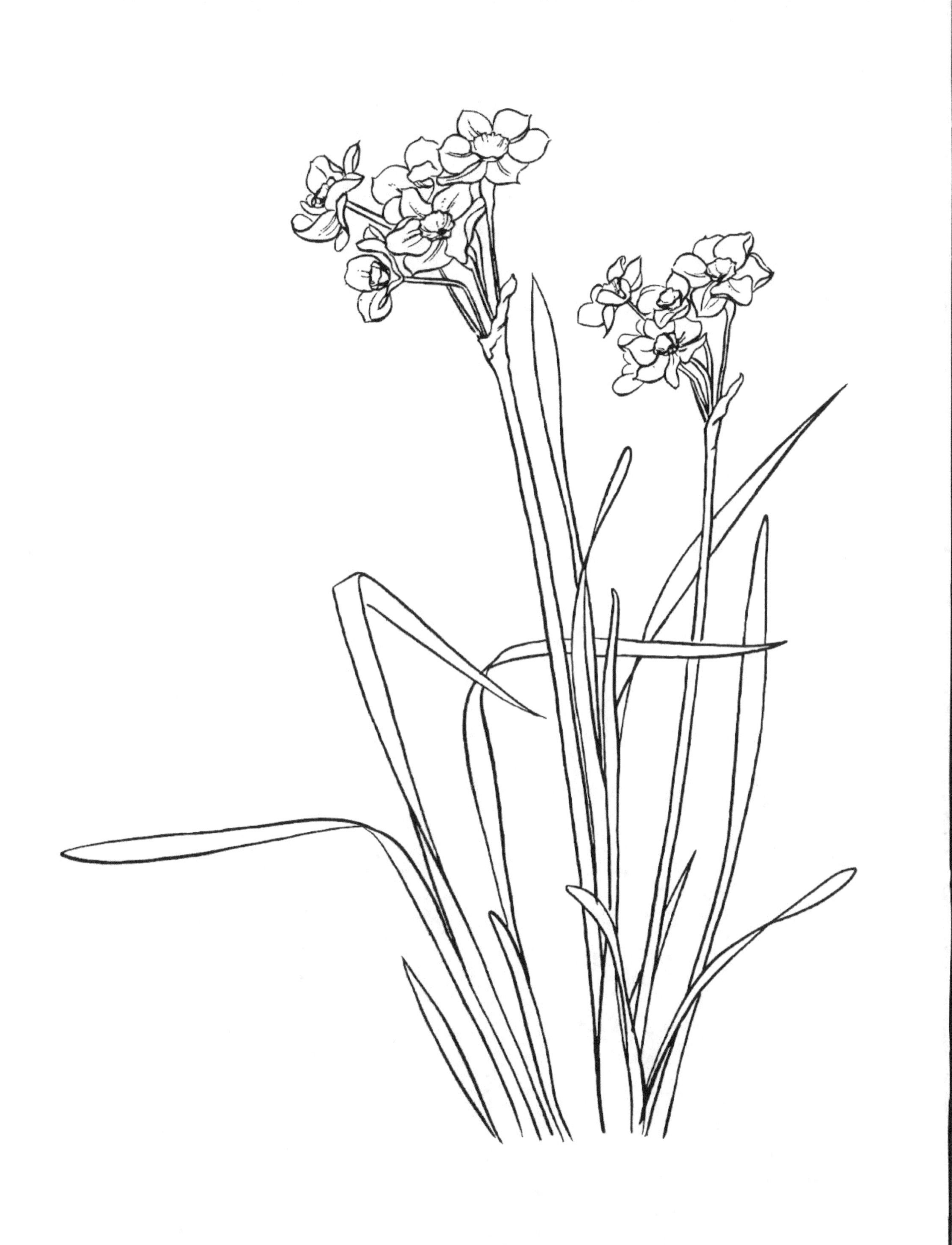

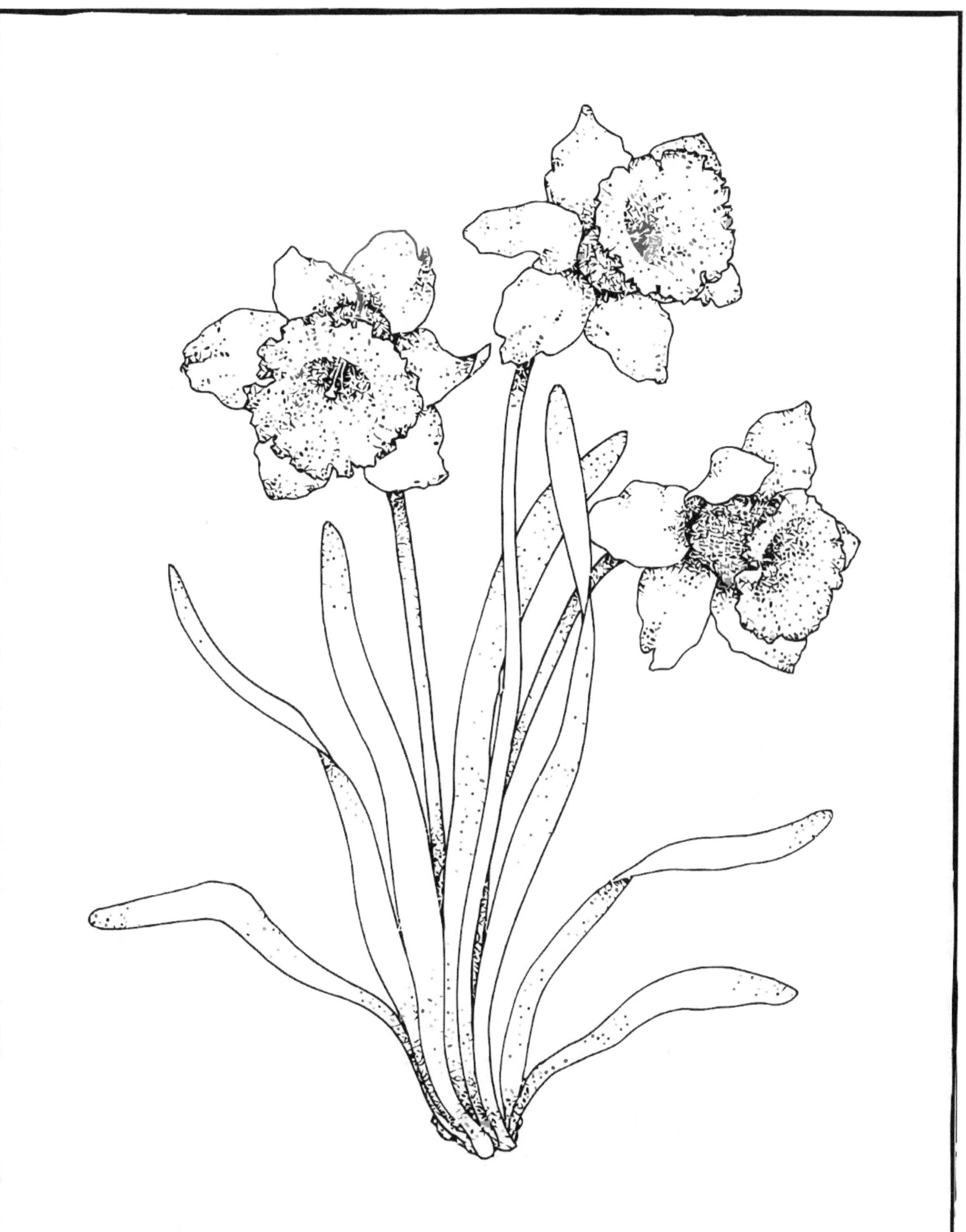

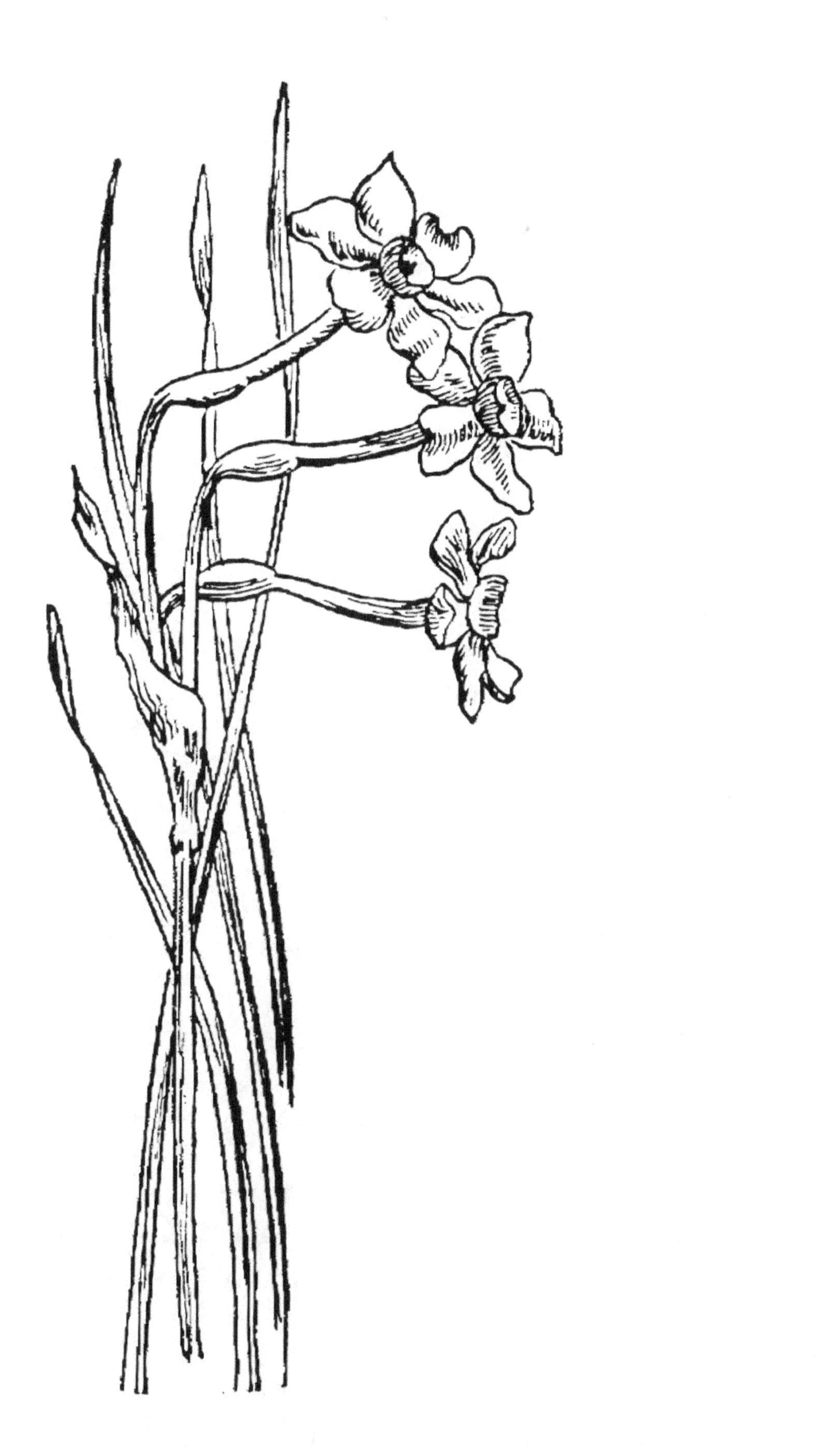

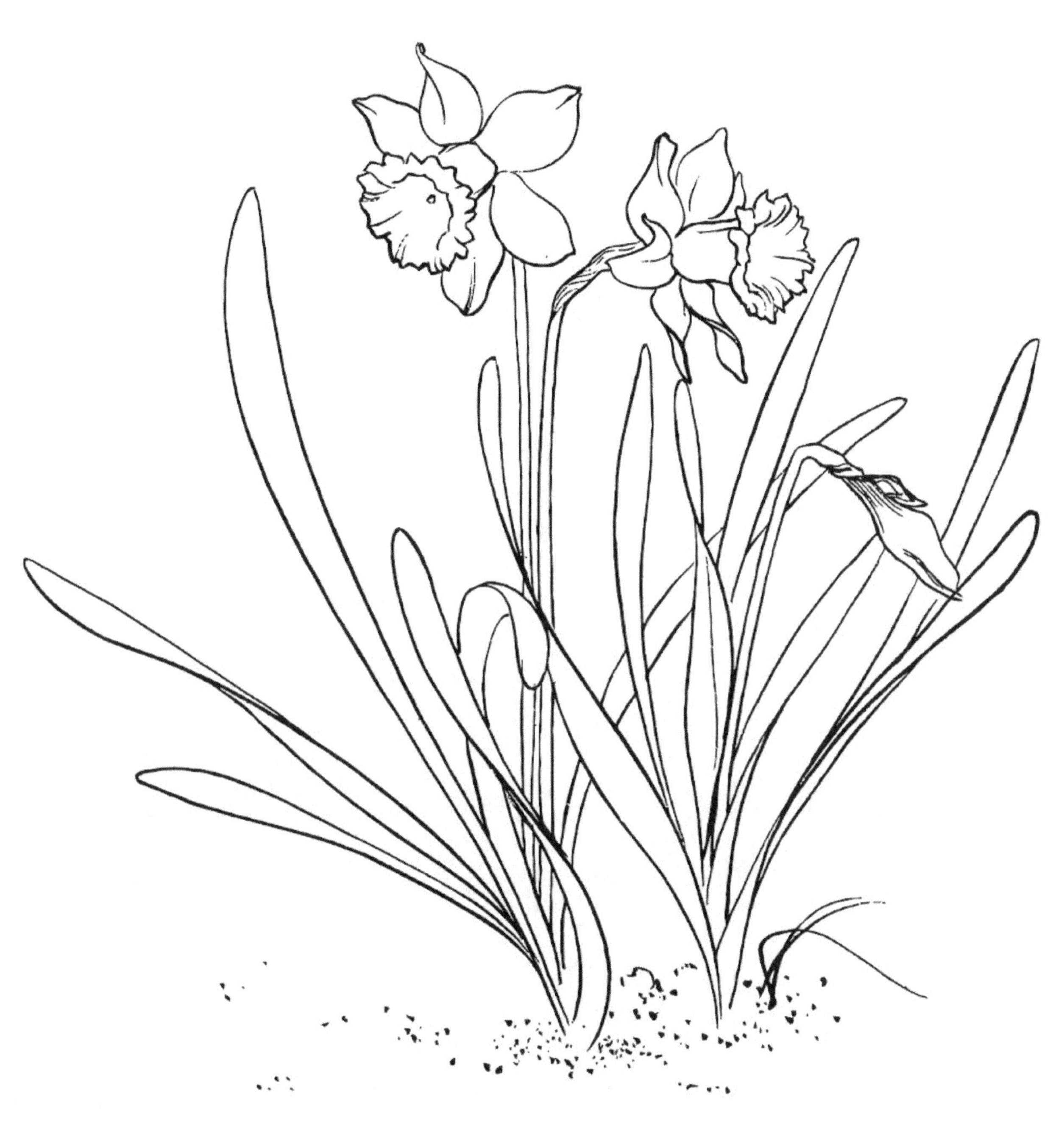

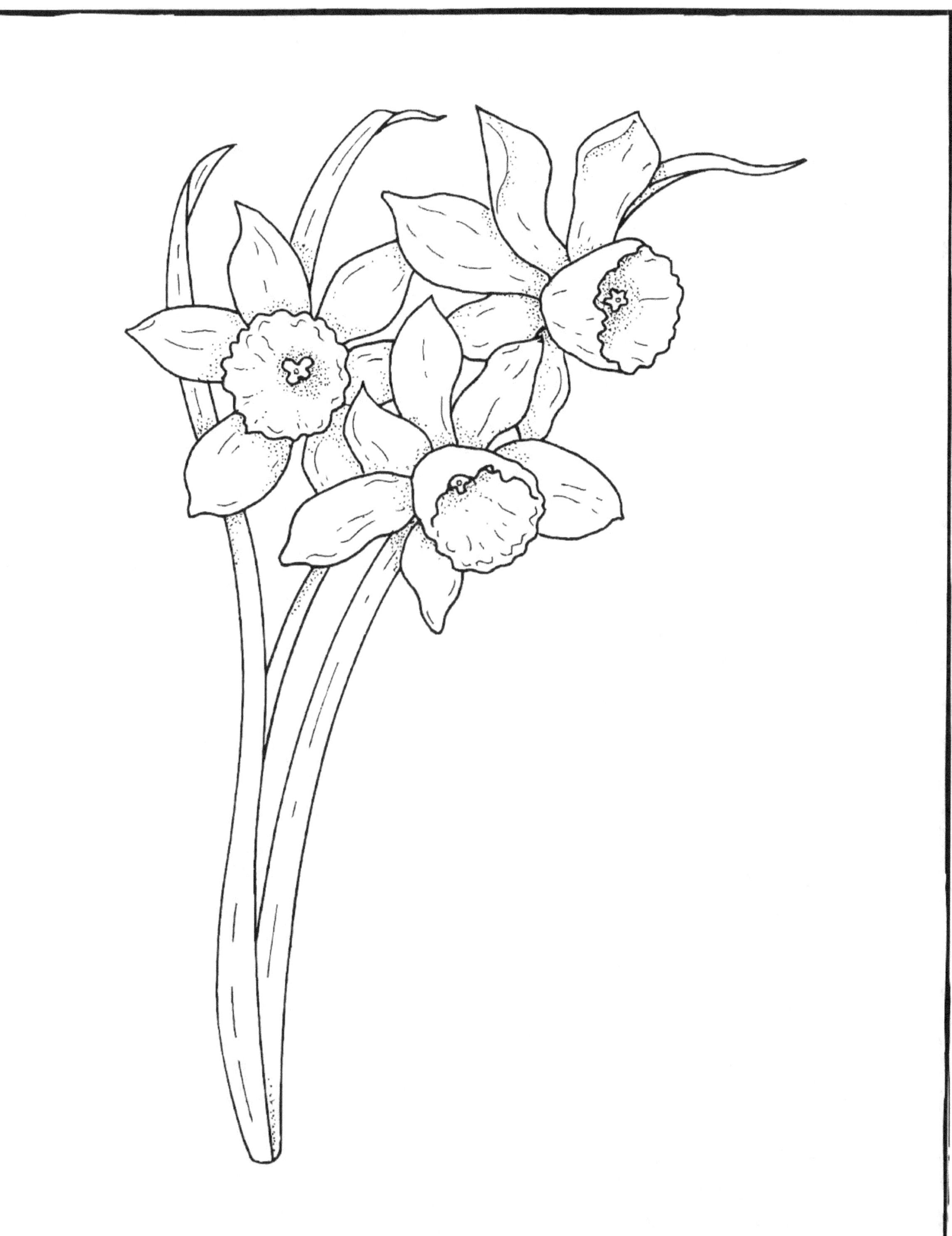

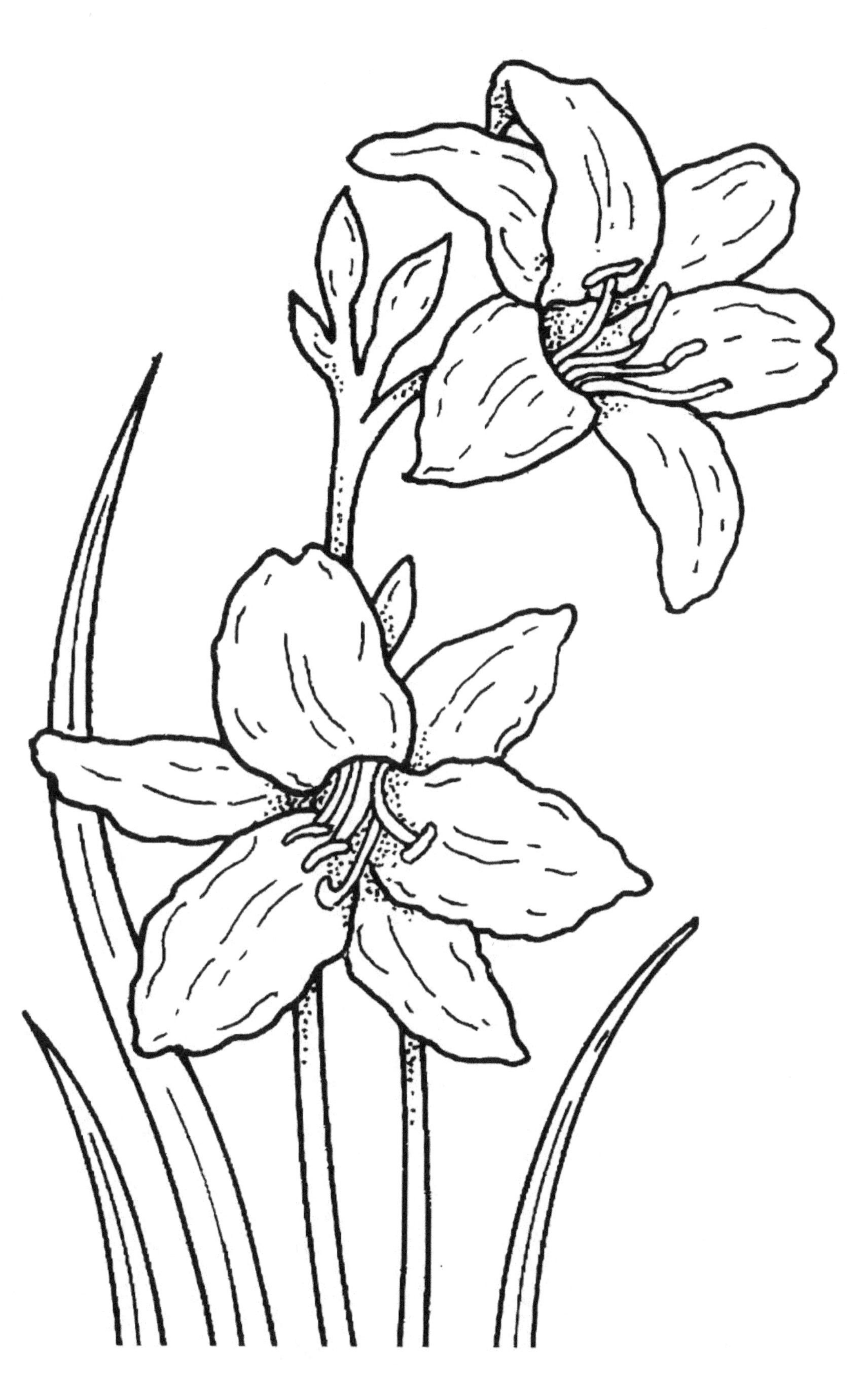

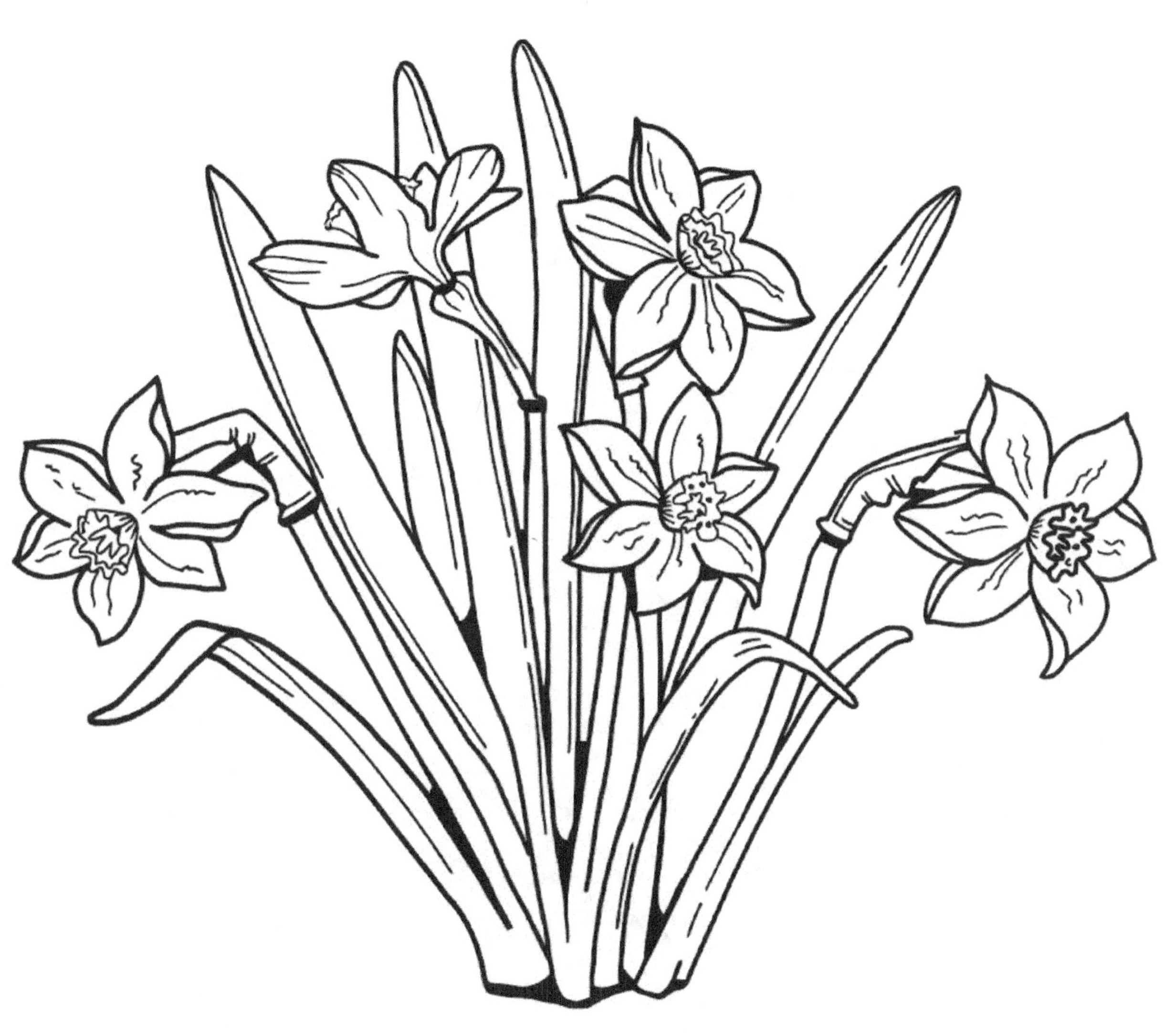

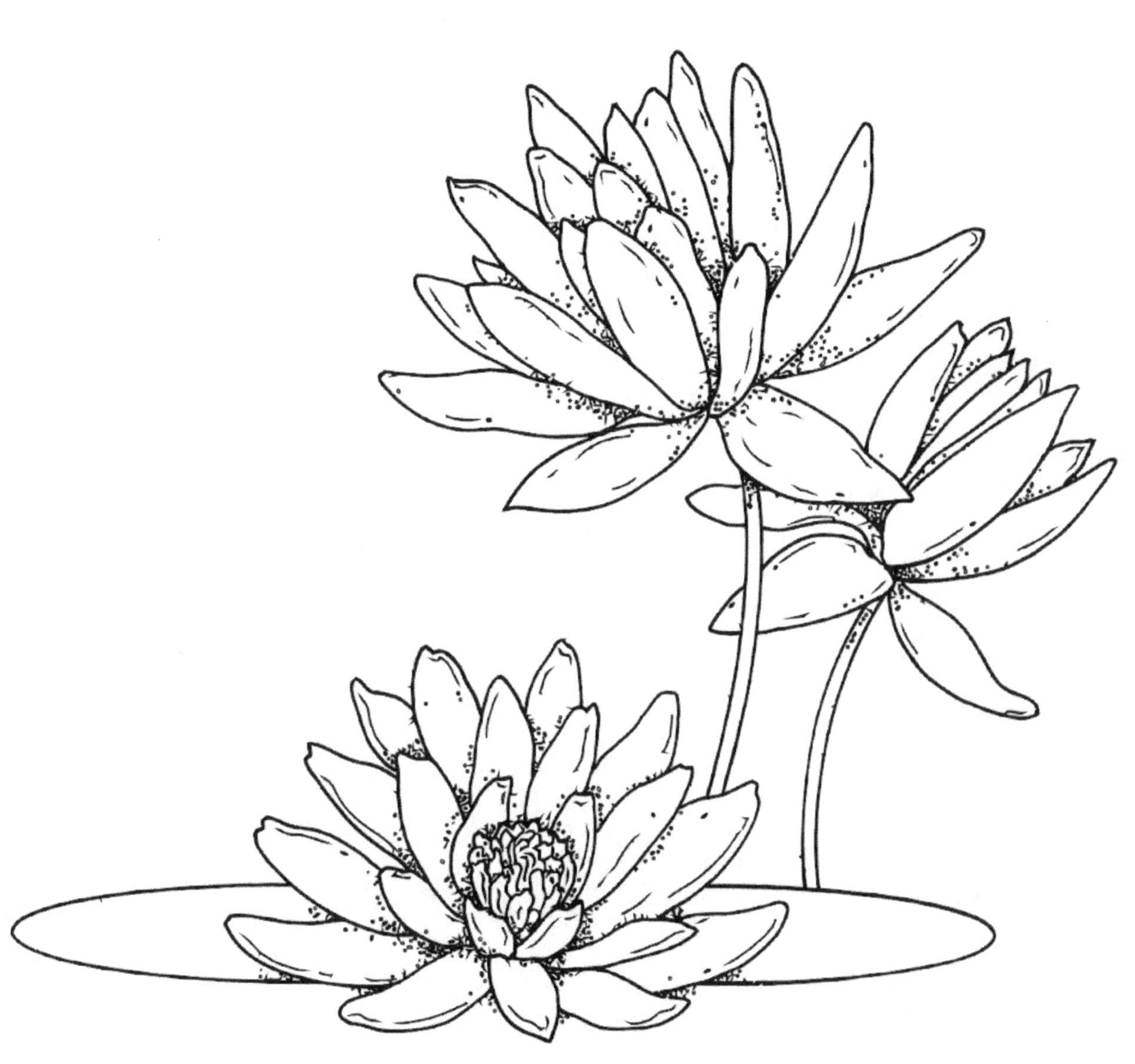

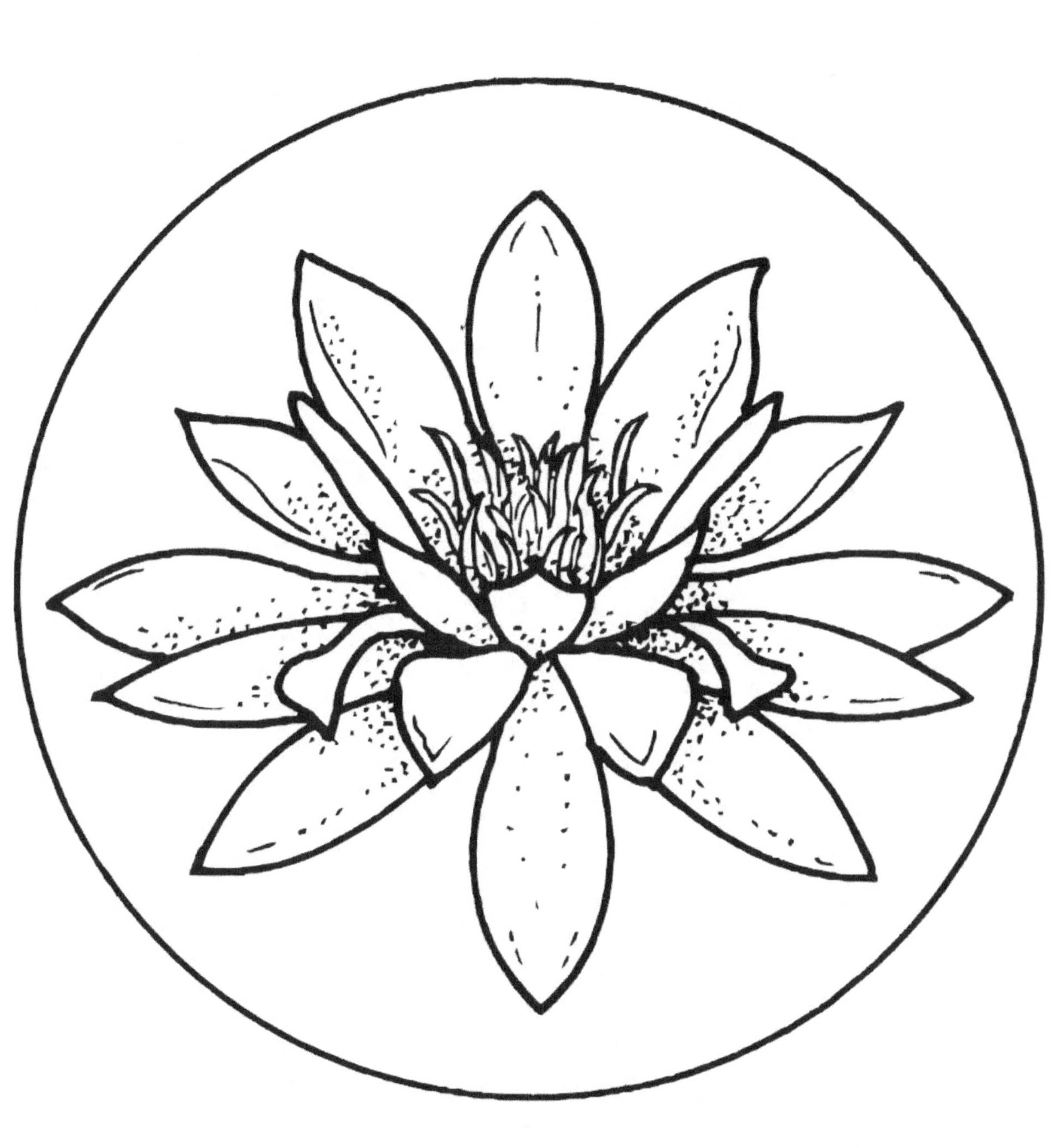

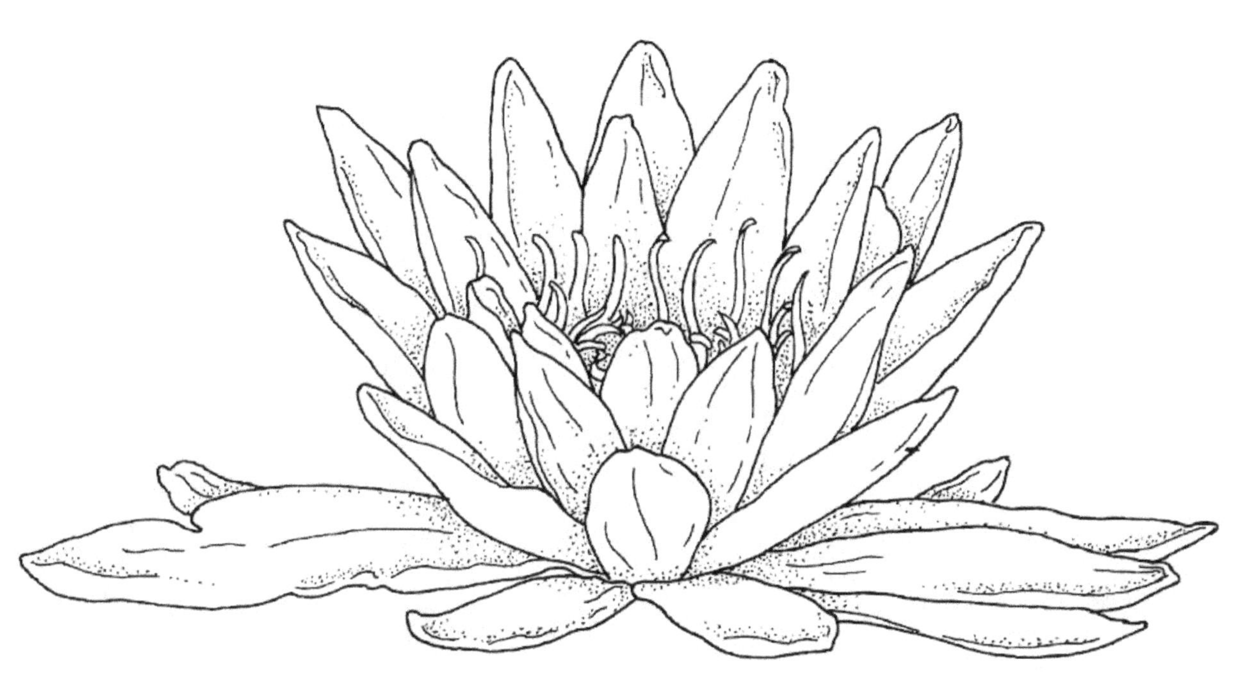

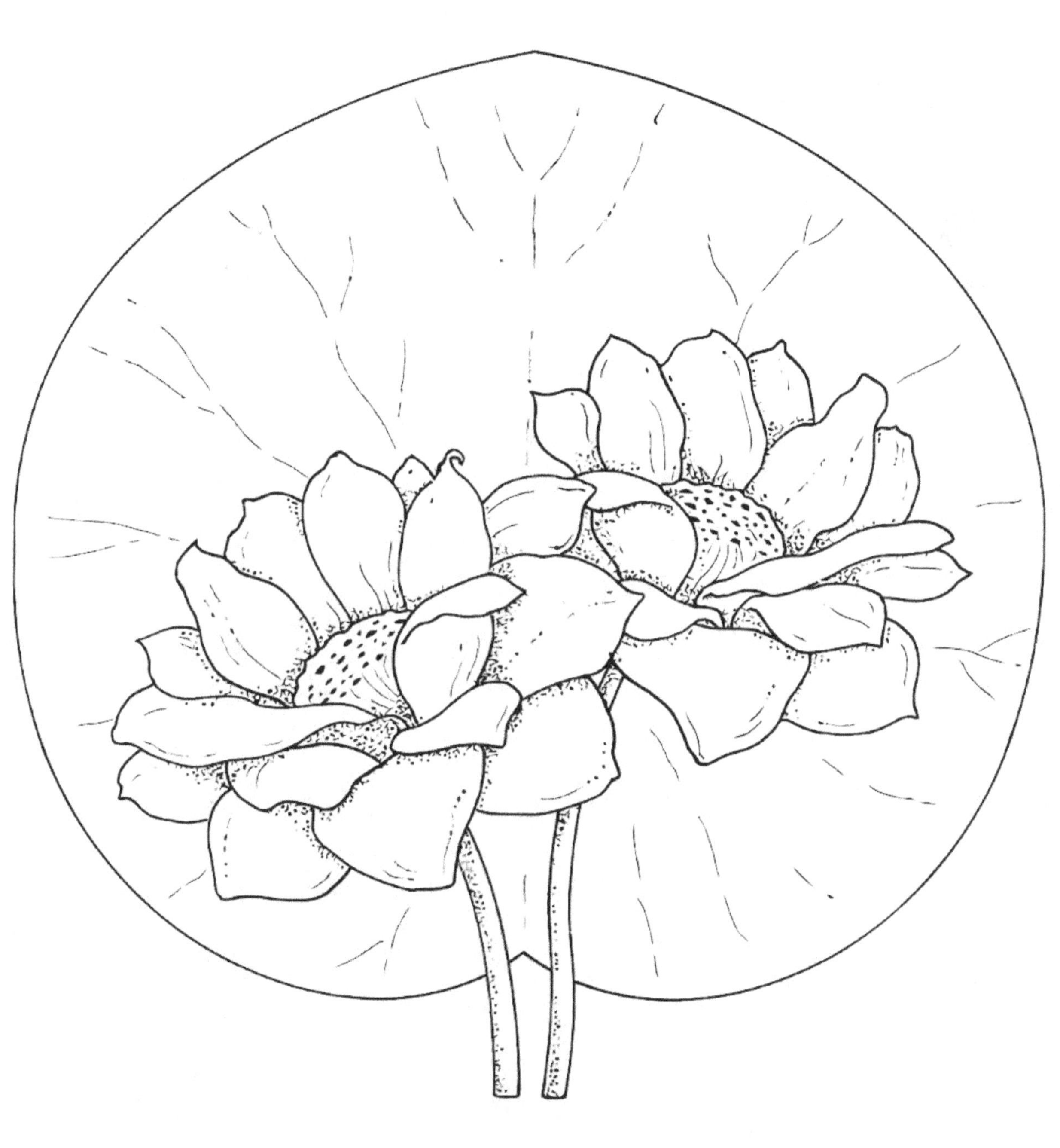

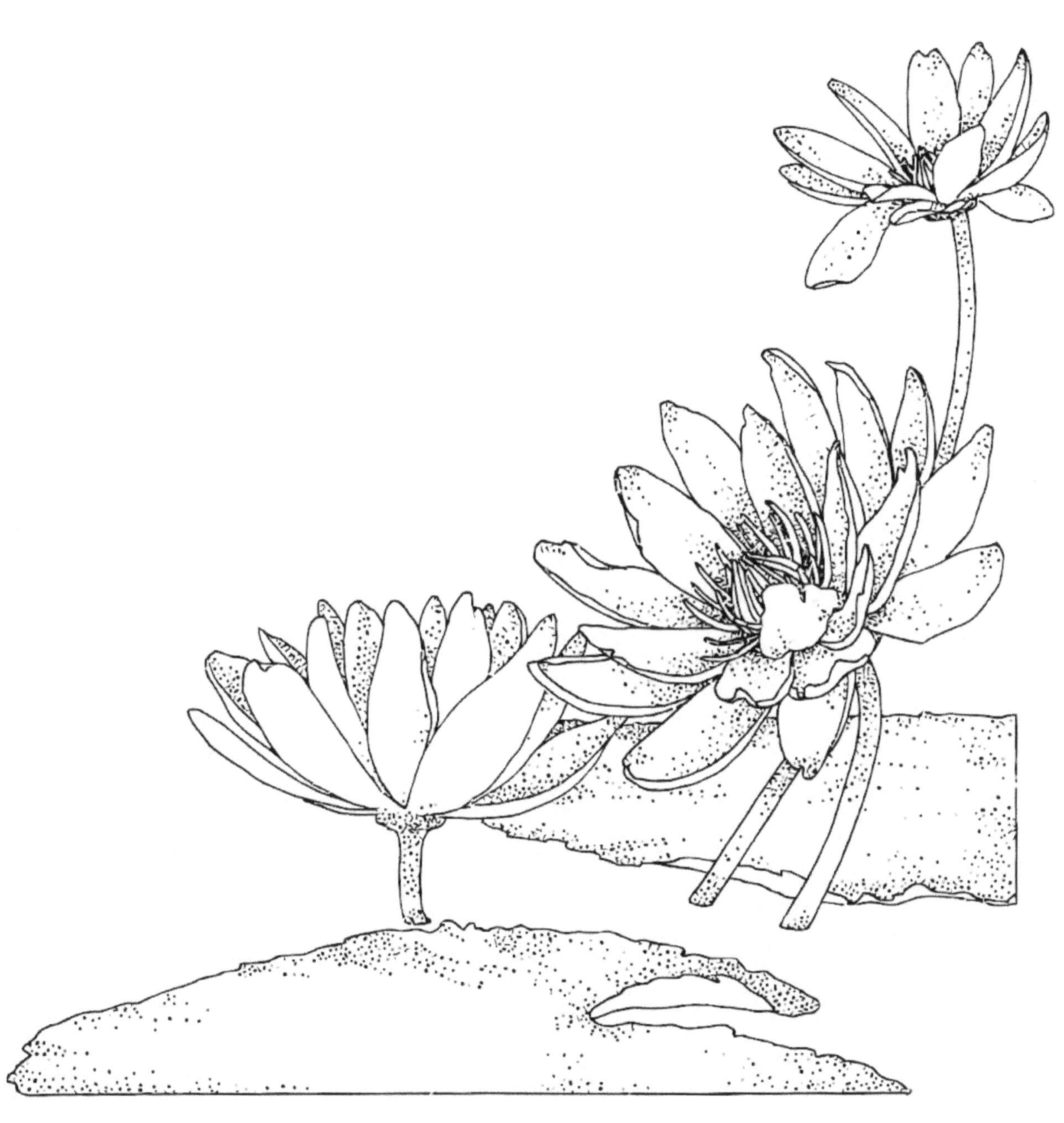

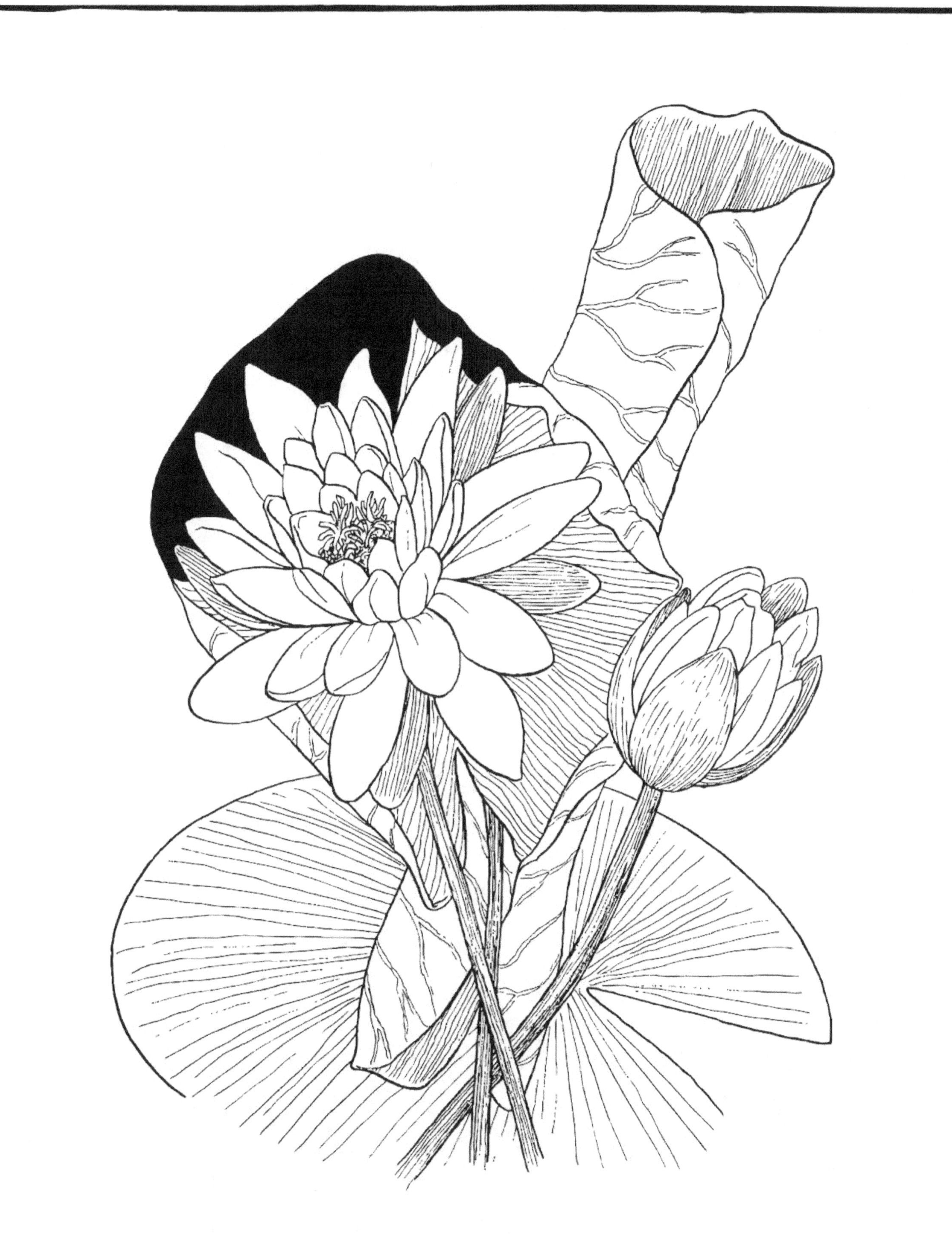

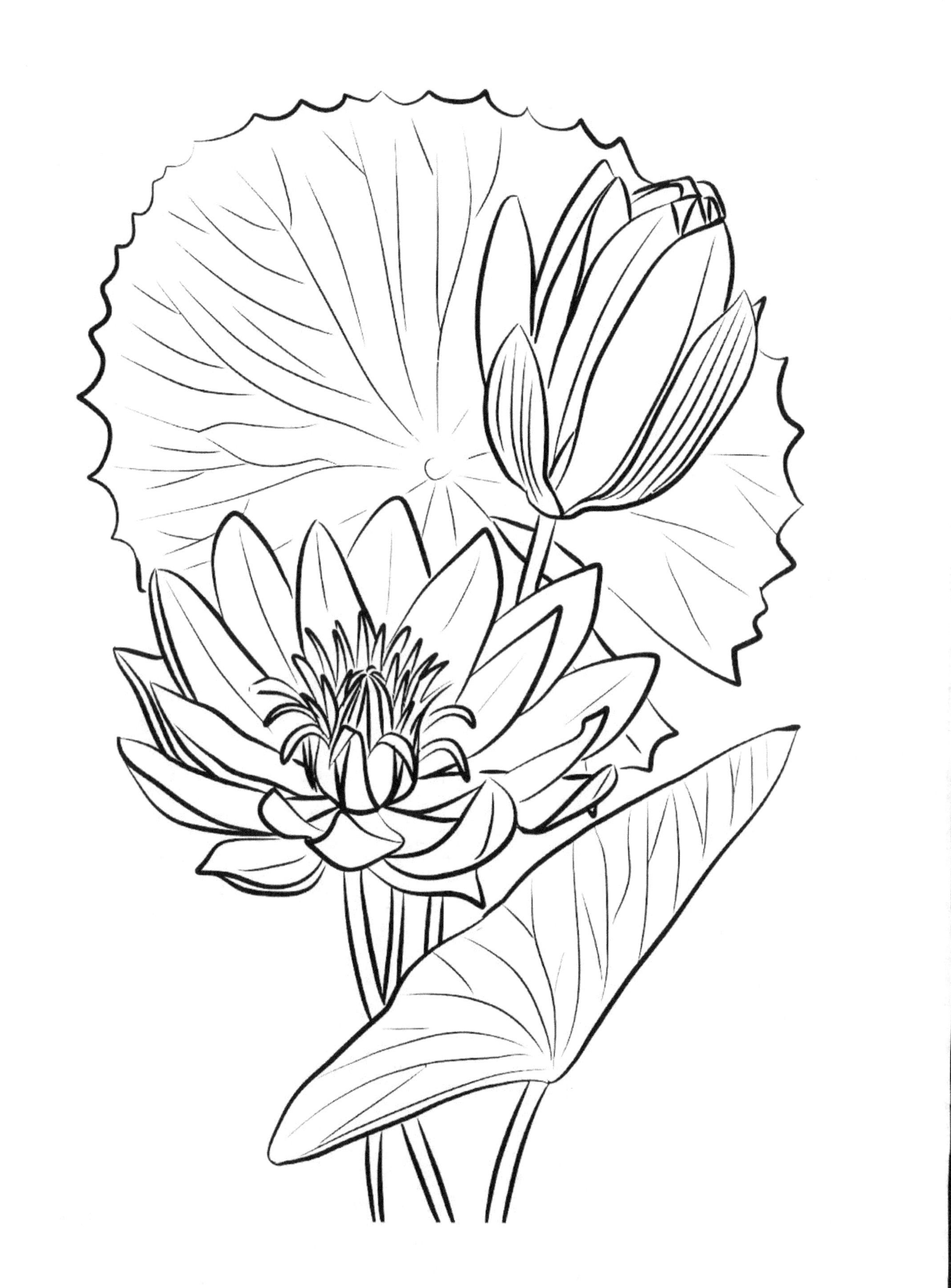

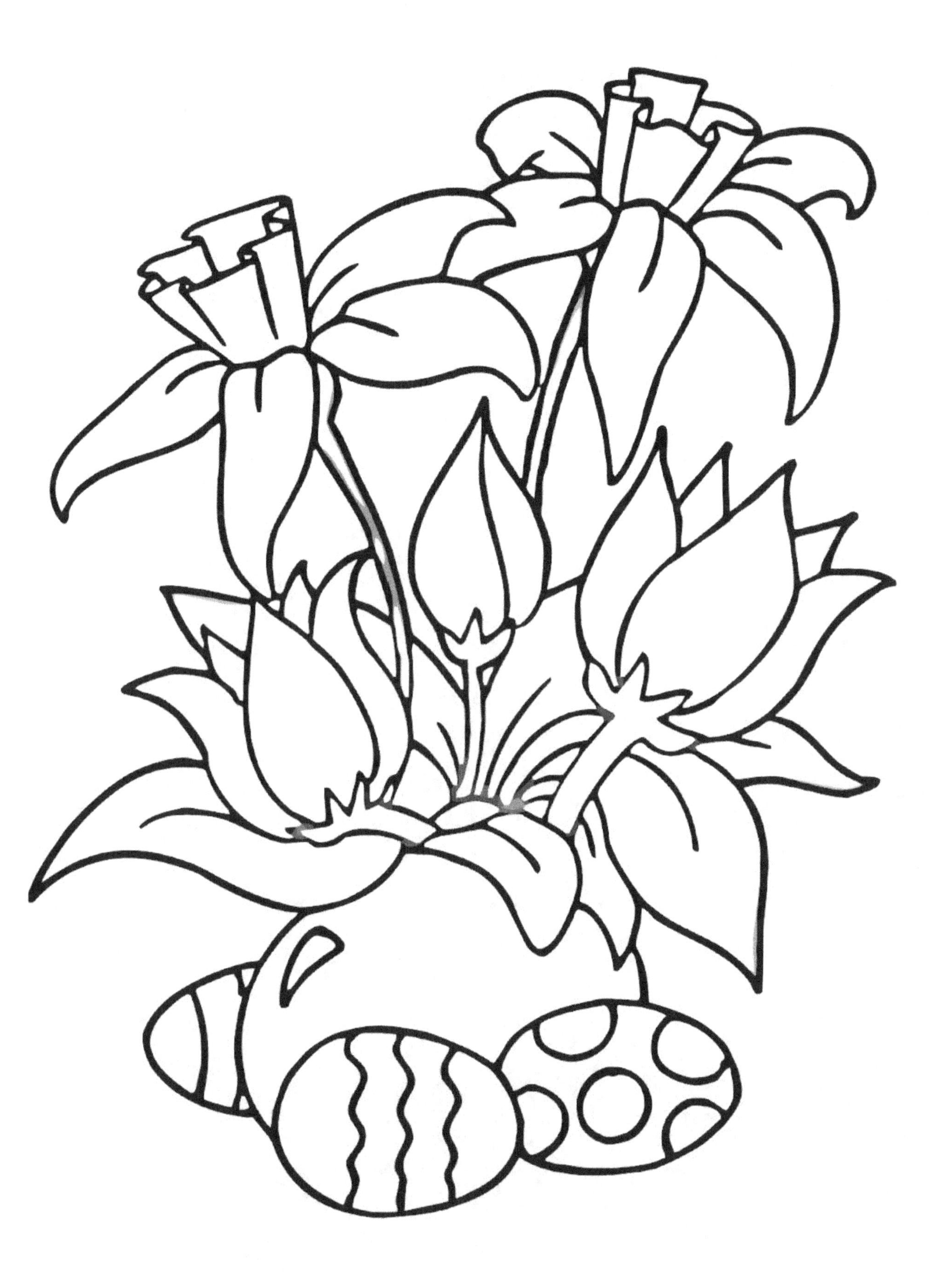

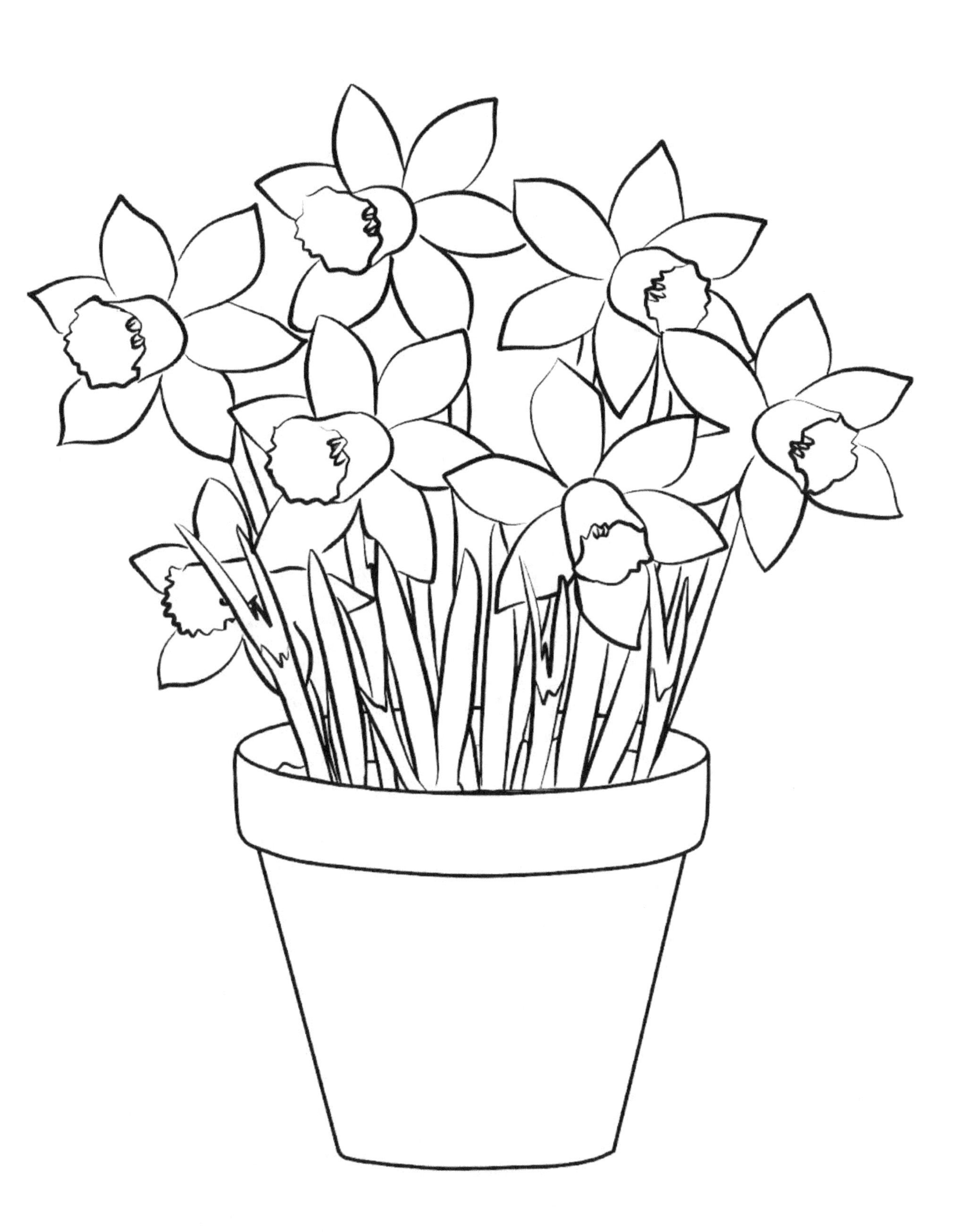

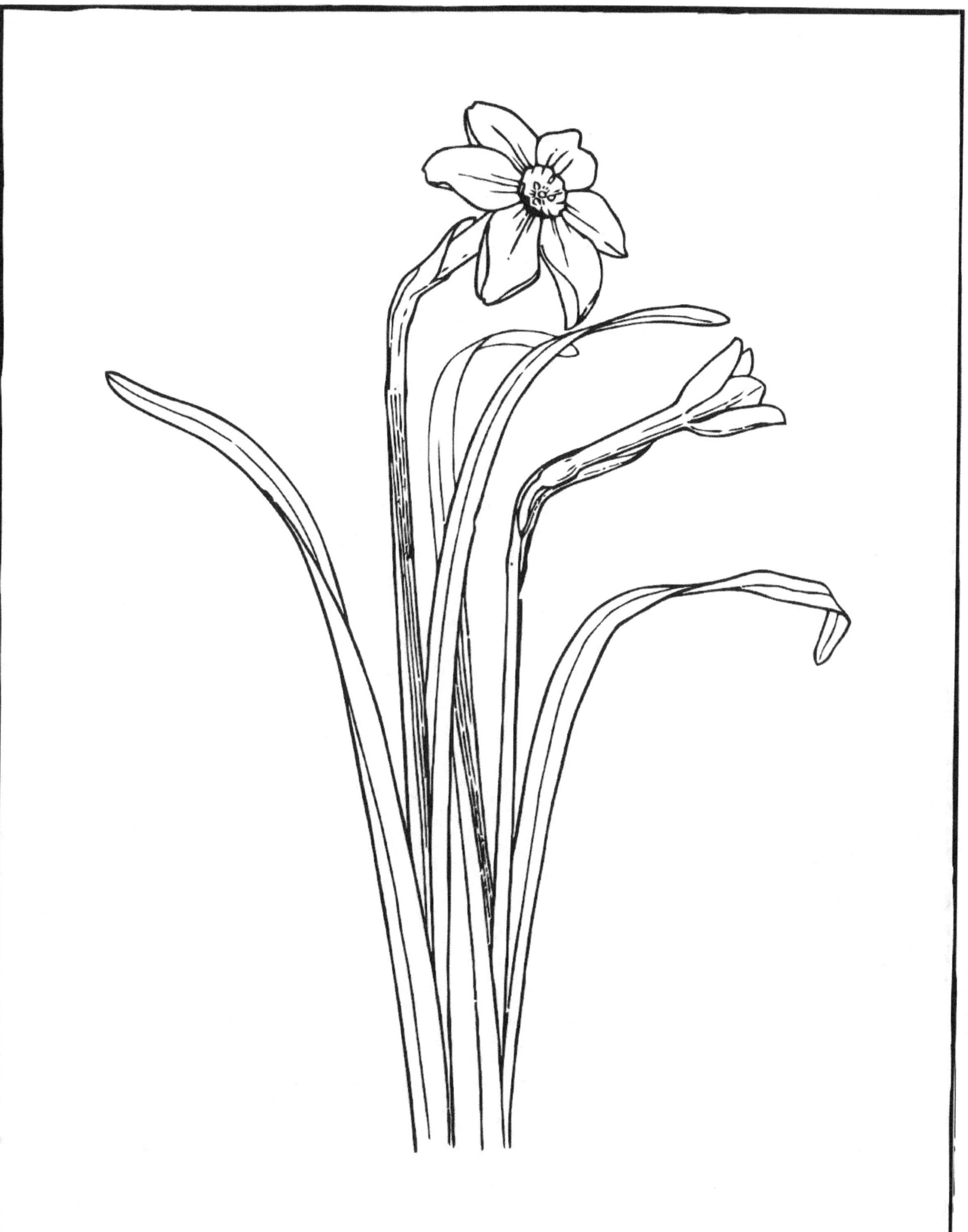

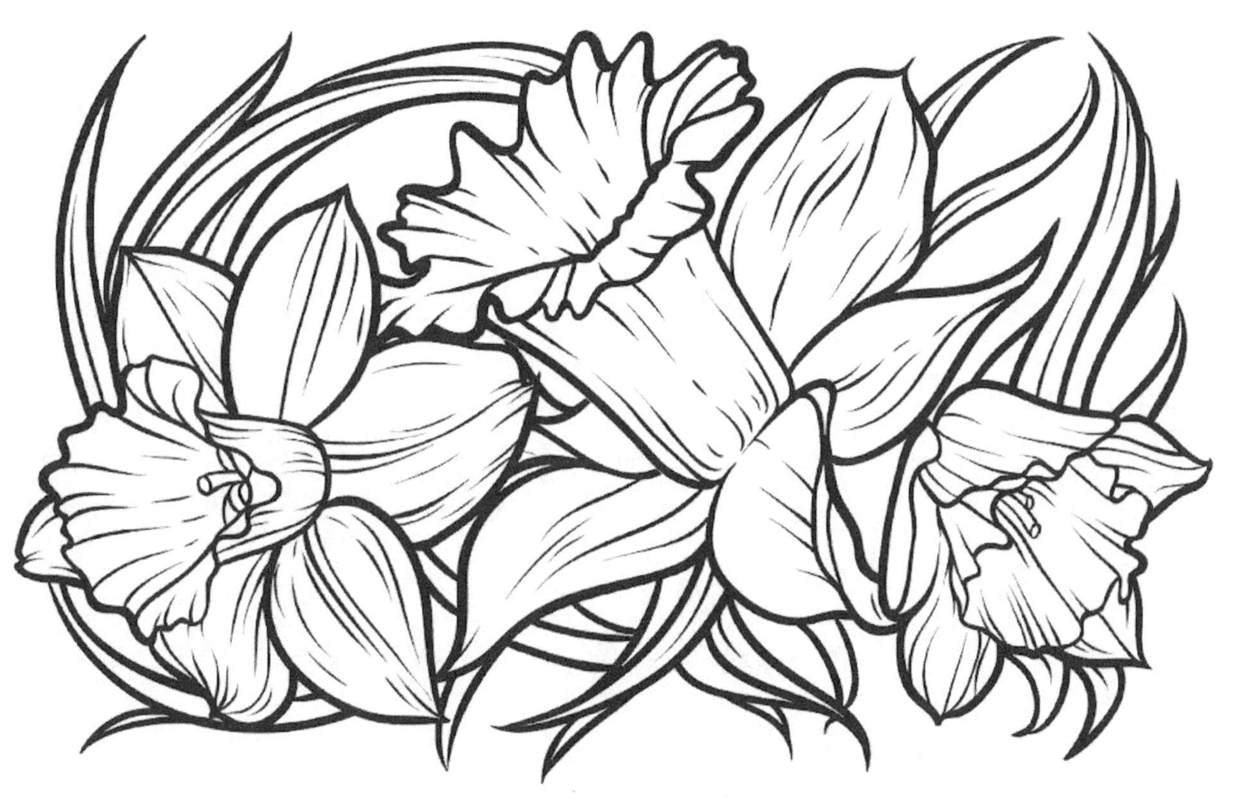

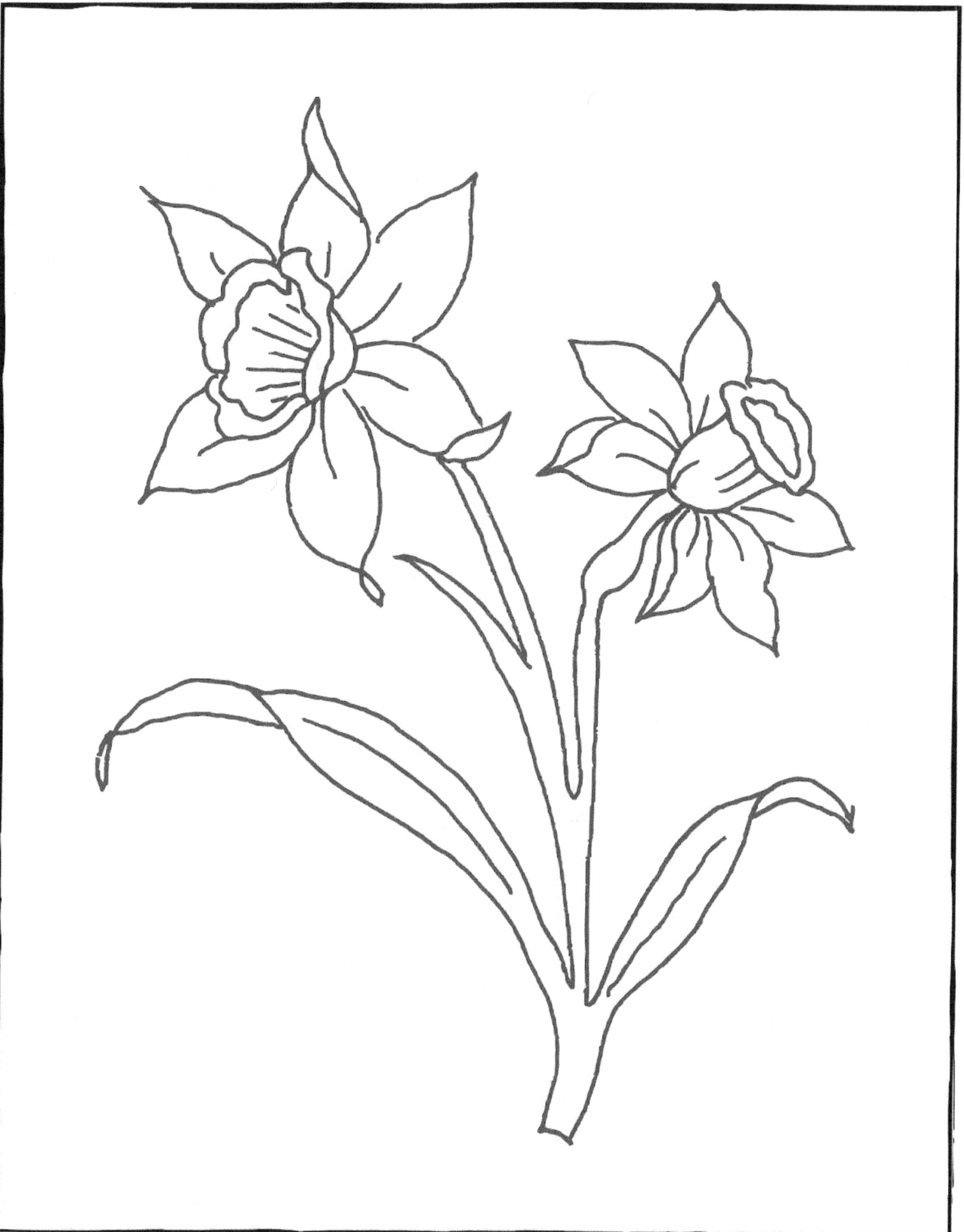

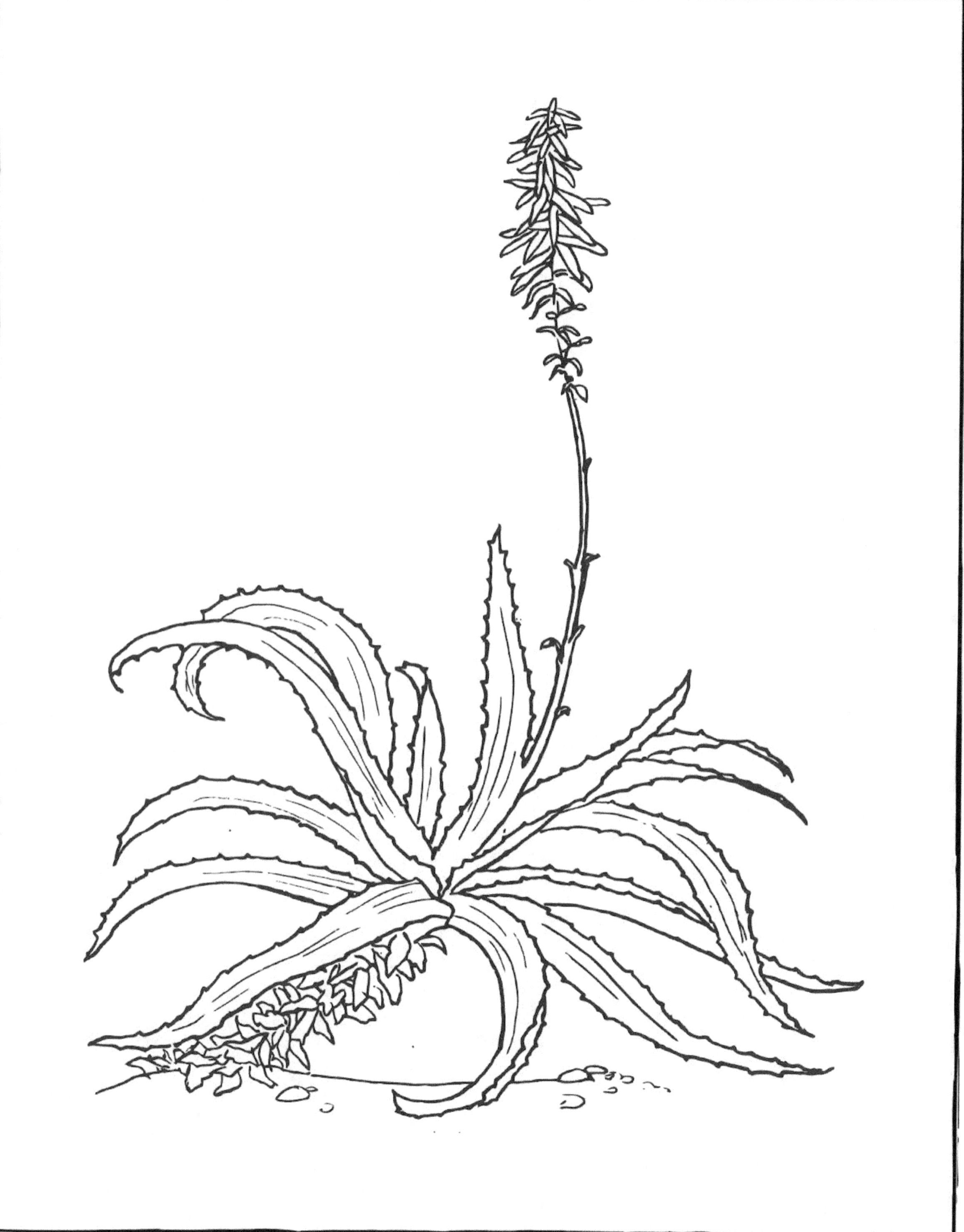

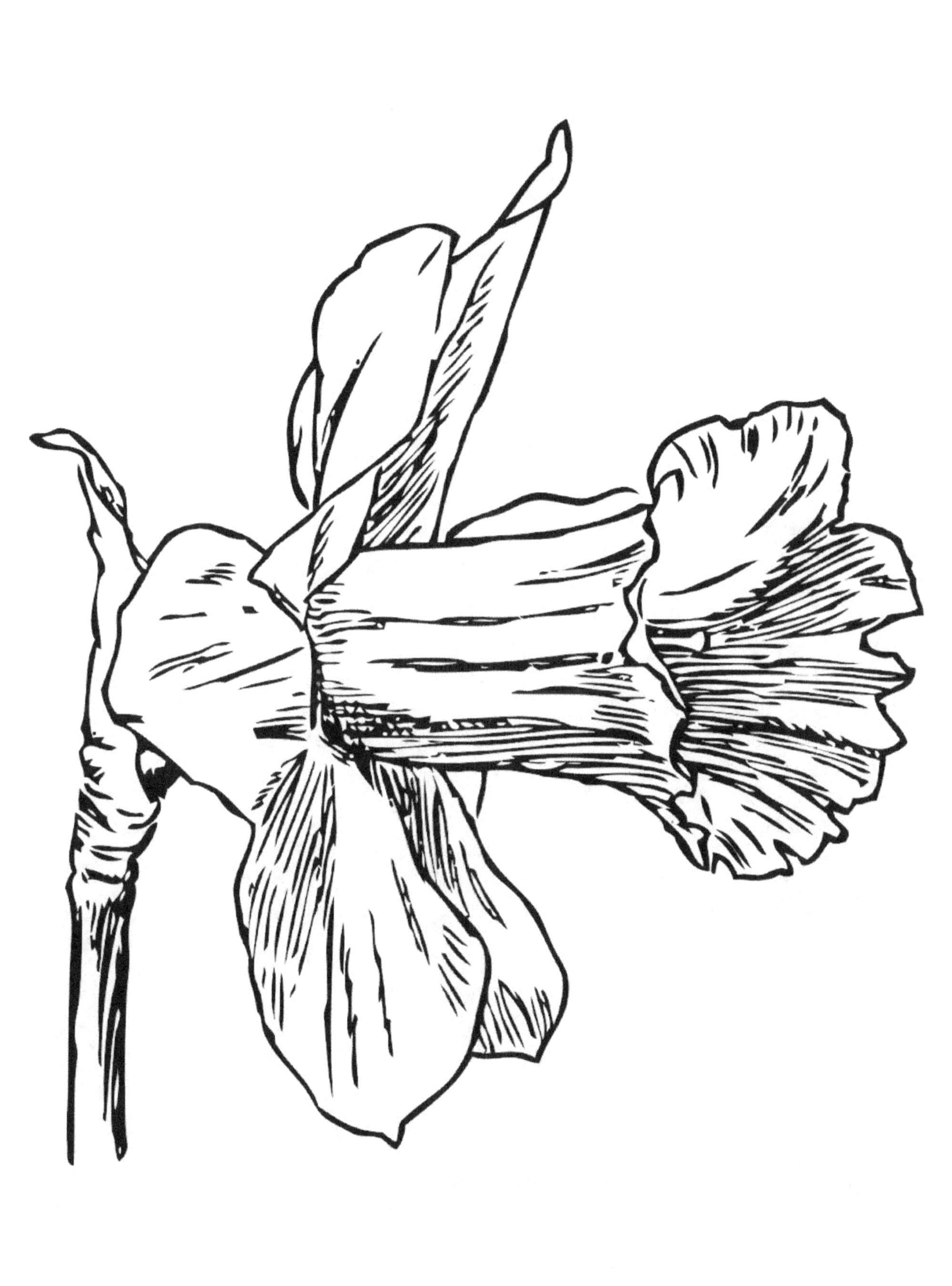

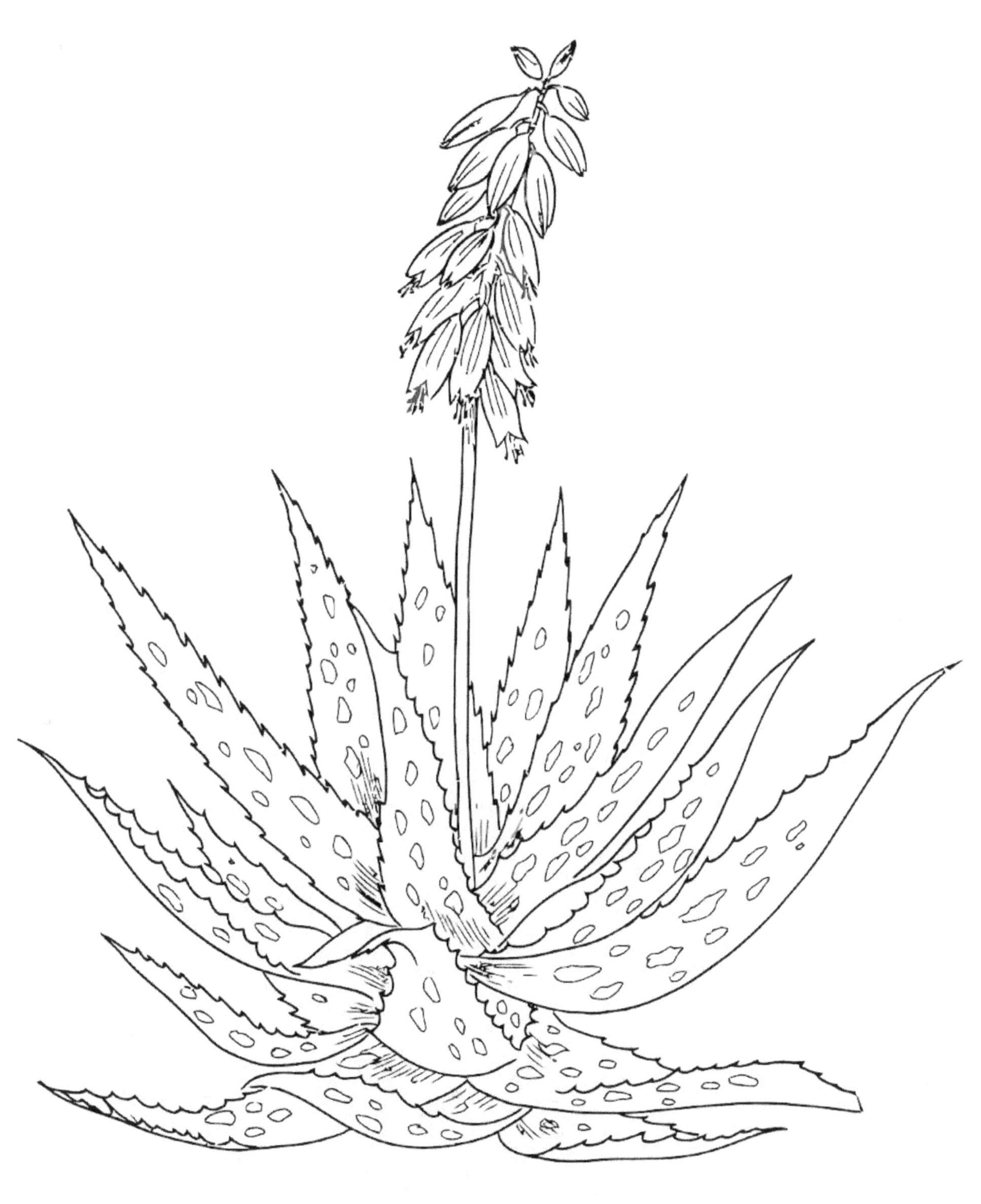

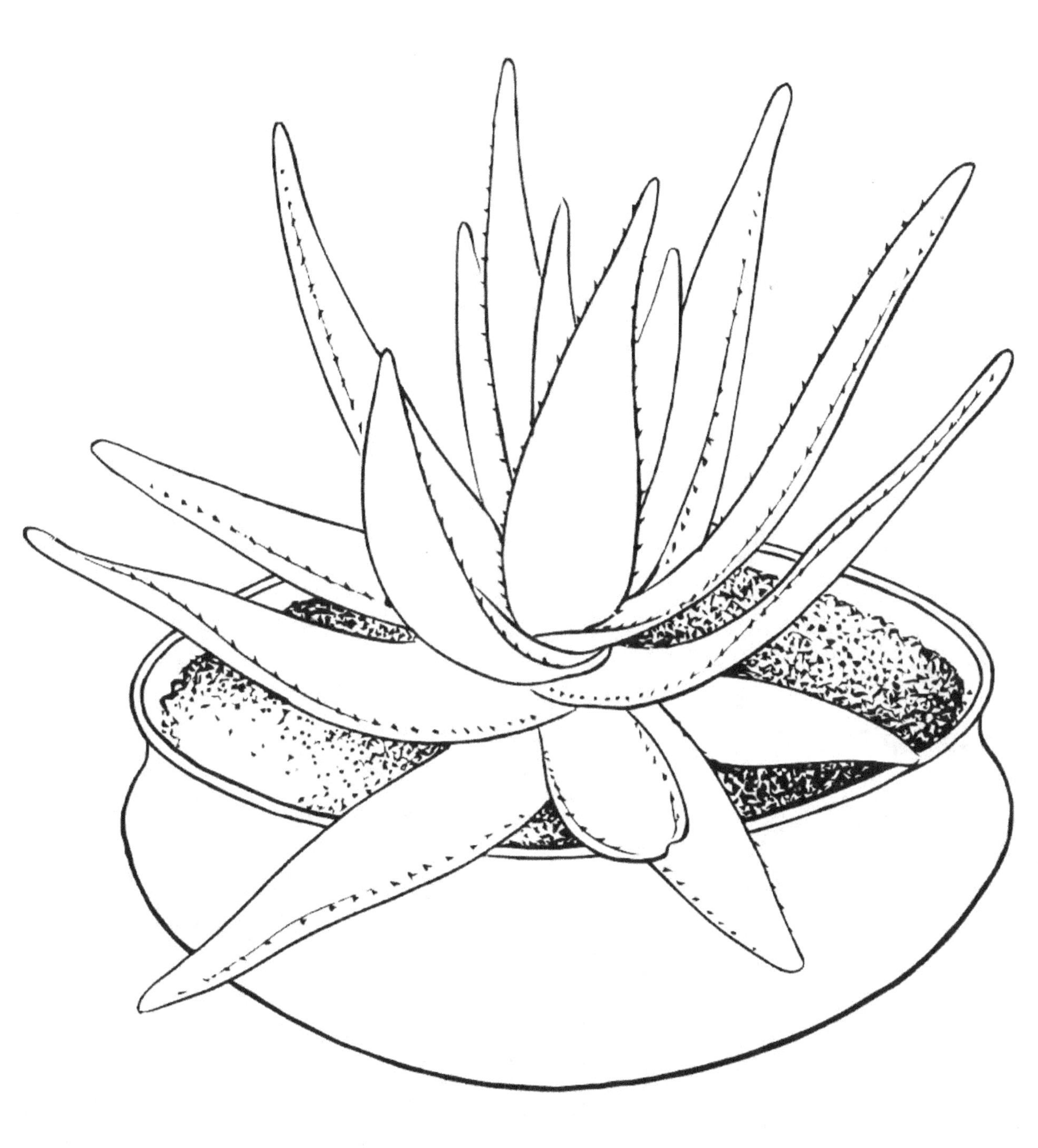

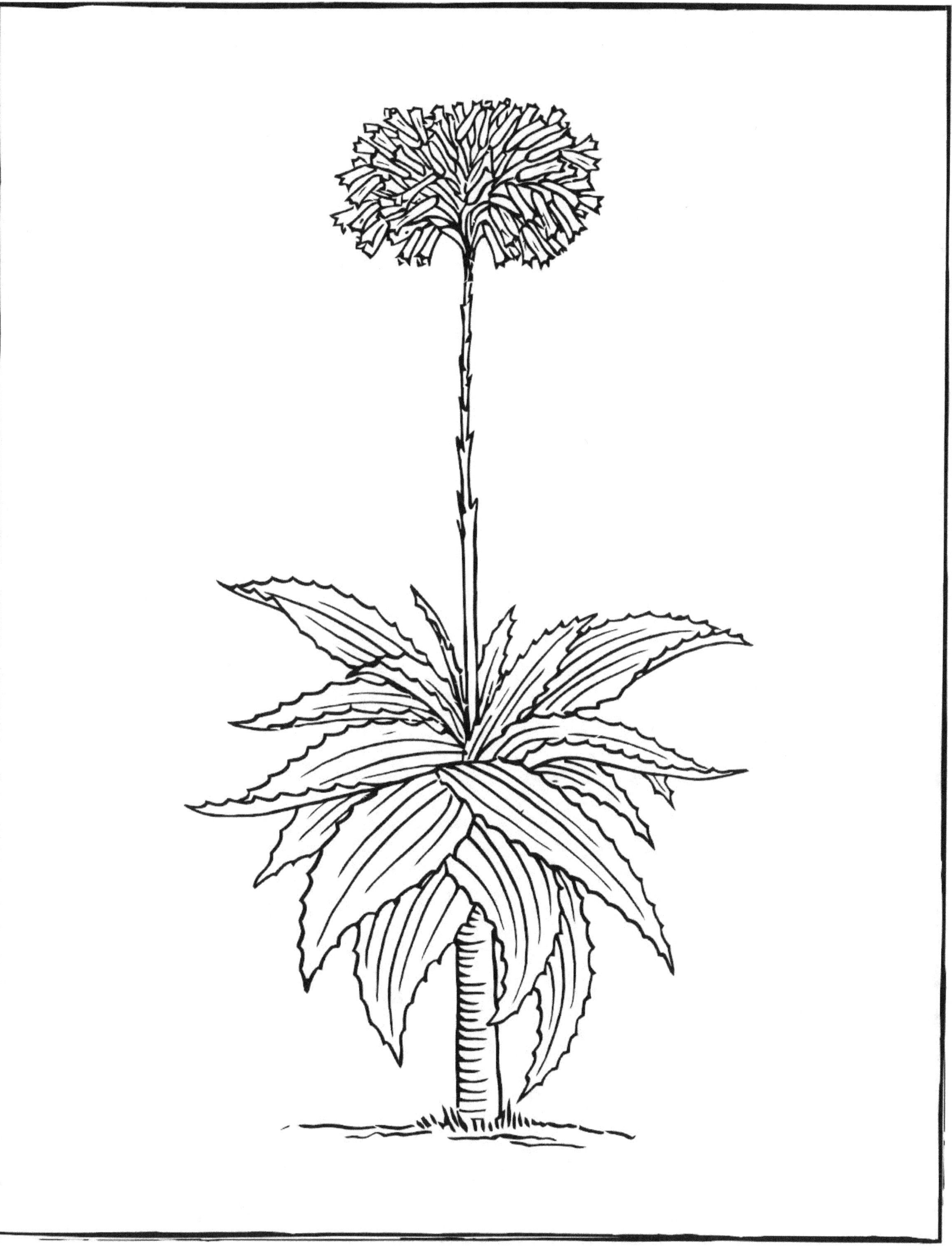